The Complete Book of

CHRISTIAN

Baby Names

Popularity, Trending, Origin, and Significance

The Complete Book of

CHRISTIAN

Baby Names

Popularity, Trending, Origin, and Significance

CATHERINE ULER

The Telling Voice

Ordering information: www.tellingvoice.com

Publisher: The Telling Voice
Editor: Carol Nolan

LIBRARY OF CONGRESS CATALOGING-IN-PUBLICATION DATA
Uler, Catherine.
The Complete Book of Christian Baby Names: Popularity, Trending, Origin, and Significance / Catherine Uler
2nd Edition: July 2015
The Telling Voice
Includes index
Library of Congress Catalog Number: 2015908625
ISBN: 978-0-9964375-0-9 (paperback)
1. Names, Personal—Dictionaries.
2. Names, Personal—Religious aspects—Christianity—Dictionaries.
3. Names in the Bible—Dictionaries. 4. Christian saints—Names.

For Hannah, Kaley, and Alicia,
because they asked me to

Table of Contents

Acknowledgements

I have been shy to ask friends to spend their time reading drafts, but when I have asked, the responses have been supportive and generous. Bill Bergeron gave helpful input into proposals and prototypes; Warren Pearson and Linda Keohan took the time to read early drafts; and Sheila Bergeron spent a snowy evening talking titles with me.

I am very grateful to Carol Noland for her enthusiasm and for the many hours she spent editing a late draft. Her advice was always sound and led to some significant changes in the book.

Thanks also to my husband and daughter for putting up with late nights, early mornings, and my frequent distraction from household matters.

Introduction

Quick Guide to Using the Book

Popularity Rankings

For some parents, an on-trend name is a must; others will skip an option they like if they feel it's overused. Personal preference means an unusual name can be a turn-on or a turn-off. For this reason, popularity information is included for each entry. If you're interested in the details of a particular name, you can check the exact number of births and the national ranking in the index. The index is also helpful in comparing unisex names, should you want to know how many boys and girls share a name.

The popularity categories are broken down in the following table (numbers are rounded off). The numbers for the two genders differ because many more names are given to girls than to boys (19,067 versus 13,977 in 2014).

Name Rank	# of Girls Given the Name	# of Boys Given the Name
top 10	10,000-20,000	14,000-19,000
top 100	3,000-10,000	4,000-14,000
top 500	600-3,000	550-4,000
top 1000	250-3,000	200-550
uncommon	100-250	100-200
endangered	< 100	< 100

Popularity Symbols for Trending and Gender

Trending symbols appear next to the popularity information for each name. The arrow symbols tell you if a name is trending up or down. Where applicable, gender symbols tell you if a name is unisex or more popular for one gender than the other. If you want to know exactly how popular a name is or the exact boy/girl split, go to the index: it tells you each name's rank and how many babies were given the name in 2014.

↑ The up arrow means the name has been increasing in popularity over the past few years. This is particularly helpful for names like Zoey and Jackson, both of which are among the 100 most popular names in the country and are trending up. If you choose one of these names, it's likely that there will be other students in your child's grade with the same name.

↓ The down arrow means the name has been decreasing in popularity over the past few years. It's interesting, for example, to compare two uncommon names like Jaron (↓), which is becoming even more obscure, and Canaan (↑), which is growing in popularity. This doesn't mean one name is a better choice than the other, but if you love Canaan it might be reassuring to know that it's moving toward the mainstream.

→ The right arrow means the name's usage has been steady over the past few years. If it's rare, it's like to remain rare; if it's popular, it's likely to remain popular.

♂ The male symbol is only used in the section on girls' names; it means that the name is used for girls but is much more common for boys. This helps you navigate names like Micah, which was given to 264 girls and 3,612 boys in 2014. The symbol gives you a heads up that anyone who sees the name might think it belongs to a boy. Keep in mind that giving boys' names to girls is a major trend—nicknames like Dani and Charlie and proper names like Sydney and Elliot are now mainstream for girls.

♀ The female symbol is only used in the section on boys' names; it means that the name is used for boys but is much more common for girls. This helps you navigate names like Eden, which was given to 447 boys and 2,117 girls in 2014. The symbol gives you a heads up that anyone who sees the name might think it belongs to a girl.

♂♀ The male and female symbols together mean that the name is used for both boys and girls, often in fairly even numbers. The symbols are used for unisex names like Jamie and Alexis. Watch out for some big surprises in this category: traditional girls' names like Jan and Joan are now predominantly given to boys, while Sidney has become a top-100 name for girls.

Spelling Variations

It's common for parents to create an unusual spelling for the name they've chosen, which means a fair number of names have more than a dozen possible spellings. Such long lists are hard to read and their helpfulness is limited because many of the variant spellings are used for only a handful of babies. This book includes only the spellings that are among the 1000 most popular names for each gender. Spelling variations are listed in order of popularity, with the most-common spelling used as the heading for the name. For Makayla, that means only four of the eighteen alternate spellings are listed. For some names, none of the alternate spellings are listed. A note is included when the most popular spelling is not the most historically accurate, as with Makayla, which is a feminine of Michael and is traditionally spelled Michaela.

For some unisex names, one spelling is decidedly more popular for boys or for girls. For example *y* is often used to make a name more feminine, as with Jordyn and Sydney. Short names ending with *i*, like Andi, Dani, and Remi, are also decidedly girly. These differences are pointed out along the way to help you make an informed decision. That way, parents who prefer Andy for their little girl will be prepared when some auntie tactlessly asks, "Why'd you give her a boy's name?"

Data Source

The popularity information in this book comes from the data released by the US Social Security Administration (SSA) for 2014 baby names. For trending, I compared the SSA statistics for each name over the past decade. Note that for privacy reasons the SSA does not release information for names that are given to fewer than five babies (of the same gender) in a year.

Top 100 Christian Names for Girls

Rank	Name				
1	Emma	62	Lucy	119	Liliana
3	Sophia	63	Alexa	120	Mary
4	Isabella	64	Alexis	121	Elena
6	Mia	66	Stella	122	Molly
7	Emily	68	Genesis	123	Makayla
8	Abigail	70	Bella	125	Andrea
9	Madison	76	Alyssa	127	Jordyn
10	Charlotte	78	Eleanor	129	Nicole
14	Elizabeth	79	Melanie	130	Delilah
17	Ella	80	Naomi	133	Ariel
18	Chloe	81	Faith	136	Mariah
19	Victoria	82	Eva	142	Ximena
21	Grace	83	Katherine	147	Josephine
22	Zoey	84	Lydia	148	Amy
23	Natalie	86	Julia	151	Eden
24	Addison	88	Khloe	153	Angelina
25	Lillian	89	Madeline	155	Rachel
28	Hannah	91	Sophie	157	Juliana
33	Samantha	92	Alexandra	158	Kaitlyn
34	Anna	95	Gianna	160	Destiny
35	Leah	96	Isabelle	162	Gracie
37	Ariana	97	Alice	164	Emilia
38	Allison	98	Vivian	166	Elise
41	Camila	102	Kayla	169	Margaret
43	Gabriella	108	Clara	171	Vanessa
44	Claire	109	Sydney	173	Gabrielle
46	Sadie	110	Trinity	177	Adriana
49	Nora	111	Natalia	184	Rebecca
50	Sarah	112	Valentina	187	Michelle
55	Ellie	114	Jocelyn	191	Angela
57	Annabelle	115	Maria	193	Harmony
58	Caroline	117	Eliana	194	Rose
59	Madelyn	118	Brielle	203	Esther
60	Serenity				

Top 100 Christian Names for Boys

Rank	Name				
1	Noah	44	Jonathan	103	Elias
2	Liam	45	Levi	104	Vincent
4	Jacob	47	Julian	106	Mateo
5	William	48	Isaiah	109	Micah
6	Ethan	49	Eli	111	Jesus
7	Michael	50	Aaron	112	Max
8	Alexander	51	Charles	114	Leonardo
9	James	54	Thomas	115	Santiago
10	Daniel	55	Jordan	117	Carlos
11	Elijah	56	Jeremiah	119	Ezra
12	Benjamin	57	Nicholas	122	Declan
14	Aiden	58	Evan	123	Eric
15	Jayden	59	Adrian	125	Giovanni
16	Matthew	61	Robert	126	Theodore
17	Jackson	64	Josiah	127	Harrison
18	David	66	Austin	128	Alex
19	Lucas	67	Angel	129	Diego
20	Joseph	68	Jace	130	Wesley
21	Anthony	69	Dominic	131	Bryce
22	Andrew	70	Kevin	132	Ivan
23	Samuel	75	Jason	134	George
24	Gabriel	76	José	135	Timothy
25	Joshua	77	Ian	137	Silas
26	John	79	Adam	138	Jonah
28	Luke	82	Zachary	139	Antonio
30	Christopher	88	Xavier	140	Colin
31	Isaac	93	Asher	141	Richard
32	Oliver	94	Nathaniel	144	Steven
33	Henry	96	Justin	145	Axel
34	Sebastian	97	Leo	146	Miguel
35	Caleb	98	Juan	151	Ryker
38	Nathan	99	Luis	152	Victor
41	Jack	102	Damian	153	Patrick
42	Christian				

GIRLS' NAMES

All of the names listed in this book are currently used in the US. The popularity and trending information provided for the names is based on information released each May by the US Social Security Administration.

Chapter 1: The Old Testament

Genesis and Job

Adah

Origin: Hebrew meaning "ornament."

Significance: one of the wives of Esau, twin brother of Jacob, to whom Esau sold his birthright.

Popularity: endangered ↑

Addison

Origin: an English last name meaning "Addie's son." Addie is a diminutive of Adam, Hebrew meaning "earth."

Significance: the first man, created by God.

Popularity: top 100 ↓

Spelling variations: *Addyson, Addisyn*

Asenath

Origin: Egyptian meaning "belongs to Neith." Neith was the Egyptian goddess of war and weaving.

Significance: Joseph's wife, who was the daughter of an Egyptian priest.

Popularity: endangered →

Related names:

Azeneth – Spanish – endangered →

Bethel

Origin: Hebrew meaning "house of God."

Significance: the city in Canaan where Jacob lay down and dreamed of his ladder.

Popularity: endangered ↑

Related names:

Beth – short form – endangered ↓

Cross-reference: Beth is also a short form of Elizabeth and is listed with the Elizabeth-names in chapter 2, "The New Testament" (page 42).

Dana (DAY-nuh)

Origin: feminine of Dan, which is Hebrew meaning "judgment."

Significance: Dan was a son of Jacob with Bilhah, one of Rachel's handmaidens. He is also a founder of one of the twelve tribes of Israel.

Popularity: top 100 ↓

Related names:

Danna (DAN-uh) – top 1000 →

Danya – endangered →

Dina (DEE-nuh)

Origin: variant spelling of Dinah, Hebrew meaning "judged."

Significance: Jacob's daughter with Leah. She was abducted by a Canaanite prince who wanted to make her his wife. For this, two of Dinah's brothers took a bloody and terrible revenge against the prince's city.

Popularity: uncommon →

Related names:

Dinah (DYE-nuh) – endangered →

Eden

Origin: from Hebrew *Gan 'Edhen*, meaning "garden of God."

Significance: the paradisiacal wilderness where Adam and Eve first lived.

Popularity: top 500 ↑

Eva

Origin: Hebrew meaning "life" and "living."

Significance: the first woman, created as a companion for Adam.

Popularity: top 500 ↑

Related names:

Eve – top 500 ↑

Evie – top 1000 ↑

Evita – endangered →

Genesis

Origin: Greek meaning "creation."

Significance: the name of the first book of the Bible. It is a Greek translation of the first word in the Old Testament, *breshit*, Hebrew meaning "in the beginning."

Popularity: top 100 ↑

Related names:

Genessa – endangered →

Israel

Origin: a Hebrew name, the meaning of which is uncertain. It is often thought to mean "struggles with God," "prince of God," or "governor through God."

Significance: another name for Jacob, given to him by God. As a body, Jacob's descendants are called Israelites.

Popularity: ♂ endangered →

Jemima

Origin: Hebrew meaning "dove."

Significance: the oldest of the three daughters Job had later in his life, after his trials had ended. Jemima's younger sisters are Keziah and Keren-Happuch.

Popularity: endangered ↑

Josephine

Origin: French feminine of Joseph, Hebrew meaning "God will add." The name implies the addition of children to a family.

Significance: Joseph was Jacob's favorite son, with Rebecca. Sold by his brothers as a slave in Egypt, he became a powerful man and ultimately was able to save all his family during a long period of famine.

Popularity: top 500 ↑

Related names:

Josie – top 500 ↑

Joey – ♂ uncommon →

Jodi – ♂♀ endangered →

Josette – endangered →

Josefina – endangered ↓

Judah

Origin: Hebrew meaning "praised."

Significance: a son of Jacob and Leah, and founder of one of the twelve tribes of Israel.

Popularity: ♂ endangered ↑

Judith

Origin: Hebrew meaning "Jewess."

Significance: one of the wives of Esau, twin brother of Jacob.

Popularity: top 1000 ↓

Related names:

Judy – diminutive – uncommon →

Yudith – Spanish – endangered →

Cross-reference: Judith is also listed later in this chapter, in the section titled "Old Testament Traditions" (page 20).

Kelis

Origin: combination of Kenneth (page 150) and Eveliss, the names of musician Kelis Rogers' parents. Eveliss appears to be a diminutive of Eve.

Significance: there have been two saints named Kenneth: 1) Cainnech of Aghaboe, a 6th century Irish missionary who founded numerous monasteries; 2) Saint Cenydd, a 6th century Welsh hermit. Eve was the first woman, created by God as a companion for Adam.

Popularity: uncommon →

Keren

Origin: short form of Keren-Happuch, a blended Hebrew and Egyptian name. Keren can either mean "shining" or "horn" in Hebrew. Happuch is Egyptian and refers to the black eyeliner that was popularly worn at the time. So, Keren-Happuch may either mean "shining black color" or "horn of black eye paint."

Significance: see Jemima.

Popularity: uncommon →

Keziah

Origin: Greek word for a spice tree called *cassia* in Hebrew.

Significance: see Jemima.

Popularity: uncommon →

Related names:

  Cassia – endangered →

Lael (LAY-elle)

Origin: Hebrew meaning "belonging to God."

Significance: a Levite who is mentioned in Numbers. His son, Eliasaph, was the head of the house of Gerson, one of four branches of the Levites, the priests of the Israelites.

Popularity: endangered →

Leah (LAY-uh or LEE-uh)

Origin: Hebrew meaning "delicate, fragile."

Significance: the first of Jacob's wives. Her sons were Reuben, Simeon, Levi, Judah, Issachar, and Zebulun. Dinah was her daughter.

Popularity: top 100 →

Spelling variations: *Lia, Leia, Lea*

Cross-reference: Lia is also a short form of names ending with –*lia*. and is listed in chapter 3 (page 56).

Levi

Origin: Hebrew meaning "attached."

Significance: Jacob's third son, with Leah. The Levites became priests and went to live among the other tribes.

Popularity: ♂ endangered ↑

Rachel

Origin: Hebrew meaning "ewe."

Significance: Jacob's favorite wife and the mother of Joseph and Benjamin.

Popularity: top 500 ↓

Related names:

  Raquel – top 1000 ↓

  Rae – endangered →

Rebecca

Origin: Hebrew meaning "captivating."

Significance: the strong-willed wife of Isaac, who tricked him into blessing Jacob over Esau.

Popularity: top 500 ↓

Related names:

Becky – endangered →

Becca – endangered ↓

Reba (REE-buh) – endangered ↓

Spelling variations: *Rebekah*

Sadie

Origin: diminutive of Sarah, Hebrew meaning "princess."

Significance: see Sarah.

Popularity: top 100 ↑

Sally

Origin: English nickname for Sarah, Hebrew meaning "princess."

Significance: see Sarah.

Popularity: uncommon →

Sarah

Origin: Hebrew meaning "princess." It is the name given to her by God— previously she had been called Sarai.

Significance: the wife of Abraham. She bore only one child, Isaac. He was promised to her by God though she was past the age of child-bearing.

Popularity: top 100 ↓

Related names:

Suri – uncommon ↑

Spelling variations: *Sara*

Cross-reference: Sarah is also listed in the section on "Old Testament Traditions" (page 20).

Sarai

Origin: Hebrew meaning "princess." It was Sarah's original name.

Significance: see Sarah.

Popularity: top 500 ↓

Related names:

Sarahi – uncommon ↓

Zoey

Origin: Greek meaning "life." It is traditionally spelled *Zoë*.

Significance: because of the similarity in meaning, Zoë was used as a name for Eve by Hellenic Jews and, consequently, by early Christians.

Popularity: top 100 ↑

Spelling variations: *Zoë, Zoie*

Cross-reference: Zoë is also an important concept in Christian theology and is listed in the section on "Christian Concepts" in chapter 3 (page 55).

Exodus and Early Years in Canaan

Aaron

Origin: possibly an ancient Egyptian name, but its meaning is not known.

Significance: a priest and a leader of the Israelites. He was Moses's brother and spoke to the people for Moses, who had a speech impediment.

Popularity: ♂ endangered →

Deborah

Origin: Hebrew meaning "bee."

Significance: the fourth judge of the Israelites and a prophetess. She led the Israelites to victory against King Jabin.

Popularity: top 1000 →

Related names:

Debbie – endangered →

Delilah

Origin: Hebrew meaning "she weakened."

Significance: Delilah was paid to learn the secret of Samson's miraculous strength—that he must never cut his hair—and told it to the Philistines (a people of Canaan). They then shaved Samson and enslaved him.

Popularity: top 500 ↑

Elisheva

Origin: Hebrew meaning "God is my oath."

Significance: Aaron's wife.

Popularity: endangered →

Cross-reference: The Greek transliteration of Elisheba is Elizabeth, which is listed along with many variations in chapter 2, "The New Testament" (pages 42-44).

Hannah

Origin: Hebrew meaning "God has graced (favored) me."

Significance: Samuel's mother. She was childless and prayed for a baby, whom she promised to give back to the service of God.

Popularity: top 100 ↓

Spelling variations: *Hanna*

Mara

Origin: Hebrew meaning "bitter."

Significance: another name for Naomi, who said, "Do not call me Naomi; call me Mara, for the Almighty has dealt very bitterly with me" (Ruth 1:20).

Popularity: top 1000 →

Milcah

Origin: Hebrew meaning "queen."

Significance: see Noa.

Popularity: endangered →

Miriam

Origin: variant spelling of Miryam, a Hebrew name of unknown meaning.

Significance: Moses's sister. When Moses was a baby, Miryam placed him in a basket by the river, where he was later found by Pharaoh's daughter.

Popularity: top 500 →

Spelling variations: *Mariam, Maryam*

Cross-reference: Miryam is the Hebrew form of Mary. There is an entire section of Mary-names in chapter 2 (page 29-37).

Naomi

Origin: Hebrew meaning "pleasantness."

Significance: Naomi was Ruth's mother-in-law. The two women had a wonderfully close and affectionate relationship.

Popularity: top 500 ↑

Related names:

Nohemi – Spanish– endangered ↓

Noam – masculine –
♂ endangered →

Spelling variations: *Noemi*

Noa

Origin: Hebrew meaning "movement." It is not related to the name Noah, though the two names are pronounced the same way.

Significance: one of five daughters of a man named Zelophehad, who died leaving no sons to inherit his property. The sisters appealed to Moses, who agreed that they should inherit their father's property. This judgment established thereafter the right of Jewish women to inherit property. Noa's sisters were Mahlah, Hoglah, Milcah, and Tirzah.

Popularity: top 1000 ↑

Ruth

Origin: Hebrew meaning "friendship."

Significance: Ruth was a non-Jewish woman who married into an Israelite family that had come to her land, Moab. Though all the men of the family died, she returned to Israel with her mother-in-law, Naomi, and married another Israelite. Her descendants include King David, Joseph (the husband of Mary), and the apostle Matthew.

Popularity: 500 ↑

Related names:

Ruthie – diminutive – uncommon ↑

Rue – short form – endangered ↑

Samantha

Origin: American feminine of Samuel, Hebrew meaning "God has heard."

Significance: Samuel was the last of the judges who led the tribes of Israel. He anointed the first kings of Israel.

Popularity: top 100 ↓

Sela

Origin: Hebrew meaning "rock."

Significance: the site of a terribly deadly victory of the Israelites over the Edomites (a people of Canaan).

Popularity: endangered ↓

Shiloh

Origin: Hebrew, possibly meaning "He whose it is."

Significance: a city where the Tabernacle was kept for 369 years. The Tabernacle is a tent sanctuary that was the assembly place of the Israelites and home of the Ark of the Covenant.

Popularity: ♂♀ top 1000 →

Tirzah

Origin: Hebrew meaning "delight."

Significance: see Noa.

Popularity: endangered →

Cross-reference: Tirzah is listed again later in this chapter (page 17).

Yael (ya-EL)

Origin: the Hebrew name for the Nubian ibex.

Significance: a Canaanite woman who sympathized with the Israelites. She killed Jabin's army commander when he came to her husband's tent for refuge after his army was defeated by the Israelites in battle (Judges 4:17-22).

Popularity: ♂ uncommon →

Related names:

Jael (JAY-el) – English form of Yael – ♂♀ uncommon →

Jaela – variation of Jael – endangered ↓

Yahaira (ya-HIGH-ruh)

Origin: Spanish feminine of Jair, Hebrew meaning "He illuminates."

Significance: a judge of the Israelites who had thirty sons.

Popularity: endangered ↓

Zipporah

Origin: Hebrew meaning "bird."

Significance: Moses's wife.

Popularity: endangered →

Related names:

Sephora – endangered ↑

The Kingdom of Israel

Abigail

Origin: Hebrew meaning "my God is rejoicing."

Significance: the wise and beautiful wife of David.

Popularity: top 100 ↓

Related names:

Abby – top 500 ↓

Spelling variations: *Abbigail*

Adina

Origin: Hebrew meaning "slender, delicate."

Significance: a brave warrior and one of David's soldiers. Adina is a masculine name in the Bible.

Popularity: uncommon →

Adriel

Origin: Hebrew meaning "God's flock."

Significance: Saul's son-in-law by marriage to Saul's daughter Merab.

Popularity: endangered ↑

Ariel

Origin: Hebrew meaning "lion of God."

Significance: a metaphorical name for Jerusalem, the capital of the united Kingdom of Israel.

Popularity: top 500 ↑

Related names:

Ariella – top 500 ↑

Spelling variations: *Arielle*

Asa

Origin: Hebrew meaning "healer."

Significance: the third king of Judah. He led the people in right worship of God.

Popularity: ♂ endangered →

Ayah

Origin: variant spelling of Aya, Hebrew meaning "bird."

Significance: Aya was the father of Rizpah, a concubine of Saul. She bore Saul two sons who met a tragic end.

Popularity: uncommon →

Azrielle

Origin: Hebrew meaning "help of God."

Significance: There are three Biblical characters named Azriel: two are mentioned in Chronicles and one was the last high priest of the united Kingdom of Israel.

Popularity: endangered →

Related names:

Azriella – endangered →

Beulah

Origin: Hebrew meaning "married" or "bride."

Significance: Isaiah foretold that Jerusalem would be deserted and that later its sons would return. Then the land would be called *Beulah*, being married to its people

Popularity: endangered →

Cross-reference: Beulah is also listed in "Christian Concepts" in chapter 3 (page 49).

Carmel

Origin: Hebrew meaning "garden" or "fertile land."

Significance: it was on Mt. Carmel that Elijah, a prophet of the northern Kingdom of Israel, performed a miracle to convince the people of God's supremacy over the Canaanite gods. Their renewed belief in God ended a long drought that God had sent as them as punishment.

Popularity: endangered →

Cross-reference: Carmel and its related names usually refer to Mary, the mother of Jesus. Those names are listed in chapter 2, "The New Testament" (page 32).

Davida

Origin: in some Slavic languages, a feminine of David, Hebrew meaning "beloved."

Significance: David was the second king of the Israelites.

Popularity: endangered ↑

Related names:

Vida – short form of Davida – uncommon ↑

Davina – Scottish feminine of David –uncommon ↑

Elia

Origin: short form of Elias, the New Testament form of Elijah, Hebrew meaning "my God is Yahweh."

Significance: Elijah was a prophet of the northern Kingdom of Israel who performed miracles and warned the people not to worship Canaanite gods.

Popularity: uncommon →

Elisha

Origin: Hebrew meaning "my God is salvation."

Significance: a disciple of Elijah and a prophet of the northern Kingdom of Israel. He too performed miracles and continued to warn the people not to worship the Canaanite gods.

Popularity: ♂ uncommon →

Elliot

Origin: diminutive of Elias, the New Testament form of Elijah, Hebrew meaning "my God is Yahweh."

Significance: see Elia.

Popularity: ♂ top 1000 ↑

Spelling variations: *Elliott*

Ellis

Origin: contraction of Elias, the New Testament form of Elijah, Hebrew meaning "my God is Yahweh." The name Ellis was brought to Europe in the Middle Ages by Crusaders returning from the Middle East.

Significance: see Elia.

Popularity: ♂♀ uncommon ↑

Related names:

Ellison – Ellis's son – top 1000 ↑

Jesse (JESS-ee)

Origin: Hebrew meaning "God exists."

Significance: the father of David, the second king of the Israelites.

Popularity: ♂ top 1000 ↓

Cross-reference: Jesse and Jessie are pronounced the same way, but are not related. Jessie is a Scottish nickname for Jeanne and is listed with the John-names in chapter 2 (page 40). Jessie is also a nickname for Jessica, an unrelated name coined by Shakespeare.

Josiah

Origin: Hebrew meaning "supported by Yahweh."

Significance: when the people of the southern Kingdom of Judah had once again begun worshipping Canaanite gods, King Josiah led them back to right worship, though their repentance was too late to save them from the destruction of Jerusalem.

Popularity: ♂ endangered →

Judah

Origin: Hebrew meaning "praised."

Significance: the name of the southern kingdom of Israel.

Popularity: ♂ endangered ↑

Micah (MIKE-uh)

Origin: from the same root as Michael; both mean "Who is like God?"

Significance: the author of the Book of Micah and a prophet of southern Kingdom of Judah. After the destruction of the northern Kingdom of Israel, he warned the people that the suffering in the south had been a punishment from God. Micah prophesied that Judah would suffer the same fate.

Popularity: ♂ top 1000 ↓

Neriah

Origin: Hebrew meaning "God is my lamp."

Significance: the father of Baruch and Seraiah, who were disciples of the prophet Jeremiah.

Popularity: top 1000 ↑

Salem

Origin: Hebrew meaning "peace."

Significance: a city in Canaan. Also a short form of Jerusalem, which David established as the capital of the united Kingdom of Israel.

Popularity: ♂♀ uncommon ↑

Samaria

Origin: from the Hebrew name Shemer. Shemer sold a mountain to King Omri, and the mountain was later called Samaria after him.

Significance: the seat of the kings of the northern Kingdom of Israel.

Popularity: endangered →

Tamara

Origin: elaboration of Tamar, Hebrew meaning "date palm."

Significance: a healer and a woman of wise and righteous behavior. Her fate, however, was tragic. As David's daughter, she is included in the genealogy of Jesus.

Popularity: uncommon ↓

Related names:

Tamar – endangered →

Tammy – endangered ↓

Tirzah

Origin: Hebrew meaning "delight."

Significance: Tirzah was sometimes the capital city of the northern Kingdom of Israel. It is also mentioned in Song of Solomon 6:4.

Popularity: endangered →

Cross-reference: Because Tirzah is the name of a girl mentioned in Numbers, it is listed a second time in this chapter, in the section titled "Exodus and Early Years in Canaan" (page 13).

Zion

Origin: the Canaanite name of a hill near Jerusalem and also the name of a fortress on that hill.

Significance: Solomon built the First Temple on Mount Zion, and the name is often used to mean all of Jerusalem. By extension, Zion can also be a name for all of Israel and, by further extension, a name for the Jewish people.

Popularity: ♂ top 1000 →

The Israelites in Exile

Azaria

Origin: Hebrew meaning "helped by God."

Significance: a companion of Daniel. With Mishael and Hananiah, he refused to bow down to a Babylonian idol and was sentenced to be burned. The three were, however, miraculously saved and did not die in the furnace.

Popularity: top 1000 →

Brielle

Origin: short form of Gabrielle, feminine of Gabriel, Hebrew meaning "God is my strength."

Significance: see Gabriella.

Popularity: top 500 ↑

Related names:

Briella – top 1000 ↑

Cross-reference: Because Gabriel also appears to Mary, this name is included with the Christmas names in chapter 2 (page 37).

Daniela

Origin: feminine of Daniel, Hebrew meaning "God is my judge."

Significance: one of the Israelites who grew up in the Babylonian court. He was able to interpret the King's dreams, so he was raised to a position of great power within Babylonia. Later Daniel's own dreams were interpreted for him by the angel Gabriel.

Popularity: top 500 ↓

Related names:

Danna (DAN-uh) – contraction of Daniela – top 1000 →

Danielle – another feminine of Daniel – top 500 ↓

Dana (DAY-nuh) – another feminine of Daniel – top 1000 ↓

Dania (DAH-nee-uh) – Spanish contracted form of Daniela – uncommon →

Dani – traditionally a boys' name, it is now used in almost equal numbers for girls and boys. The spelling *Dani* is used almost exclusively for girls and *Danny* is used almost exclusively for boys. – ♂♀ uncommon ↑

Spelling variations: *Daniella*

Esther

Origin: a Persian name, possibly related to Ishtar, Babylonian goddess of love.

Significance: Esther became the queen of Persia and saved the Israelites of the Persian Empire from being killed under a plot of the prime minister, Haman. The anniversary of this event is celebrated each year at the Jewish holiday Purim.

Popularity: top 500 ↑

Ezra

Origin: Hebrew meaning "help."

Significance: Ezra led a group of exiles back to Jerusalem and convinced them to return to right worship.

Popularity: ♂ uncommon ↑

Gabriella

Origin: feminine of Gabriel, Hebrew meaning "God is my strength."

Significance: the name of the angel who appeared to Daniel to tell him the meanings of his visions.

Popularity: top 100 ↓

Related names:

Gabrielle – top 500 ↓

Gabby – endangered →

Spelling variations: *Gabriela*

Cross-reference: Because Gabriel also appears to Mary, this name is included with the Christmas names in chapter 2, "The New Testament" (page 38).

Jayden

Origin: Hebrew, possibly meaning "He judges."

Significance: variant spelling of Jadon, mentioned in the Book of Nehemiah as one of the men who worked to rebuild the walls of Jerusalem after the exile of the Israelites had ended.

Popularity: ♂ top 1000 ↓

Joelle

Origin: feminine of Joel, Hebrew meaning "Yahweh is God."

Significance: Joel was the author of the Book of Joel. He was a prophet who commanded the people to repent and foretold future blessings.

Popularity: uncommon →

Related names:

Joella – endangered ↑

Kayla

Origin: short form of Makayla.

Significance: see Makayla.

Popularity: top 500 ↓

Spelling variations: *Keyla*

Cross-reference: Kayla is also listed in the last section of this chapter, (page 21) and in chapter 3 (page 52).

Maite (my-TEH)

Origin: Basque contraction of Maria Esther.

Significance: see Esther.

Popularity: uncommon →

Cross-reference: Maite is listed also with the Mary-names (page 35) and the saints' names (page 92).

Makayla

Origin: alternate spelling of Michaela, the Germanic feminine of Michael, Hebrew meaning "Who is like God?"

Significance: Michael was an archangel who, in a vision of Daniel's, is identified as the one who will protect Israel at the end of days.

Popularity: top 500 ↓

Spelling variations: *Mikayla, Michaela, Mikaela, Mckayla*

Cross-reference: Because Michael is important to the Book of Revelation, Makayla is also listed in "Christian Concepts" in chapter 3 (page 53).

Michelle

Origin: French feminine of Michael, Hebrew meaning "Who is like God?"

Significance: see Makayla.

Popularity: top 500 ↓

Related names:

Misha – nickname for Mikhail, the Russian form of Michael. In Russia, it's traditionally a boys' name; in the US, however, it's much more common for girls. – endangered ↑

Cross-reference: Because Michael is important to the Book of Revelation, Michelle is also listed in "Christian Concepts" in chapter 3 (page 53).

Vanessa

Origin: Jonathan Swift coined this name for a student, Esther Vanhomrigh, combining Van from her last name with Essa, a nickname for Esther.

Significance: see Esther.

Popularity: top 500 ↓

Old Testament Traditions

Figures from the Book of Tobit and the Book of Judith are included in this section. These books are part of the Catholic and Orthodox cannons, but are not canonical to Protestants. The same is true of Susanna, a figure in Catholic and Orthodox versions of the Book of Daniel, but not included Protestant versions. This section also includes Lilith, a name from Jewish traditions.

Azaria

Origin: Hebrew meaning "helped by God."

Significance: in the Book of Tobit, the angel Raphael gave Azaria as his name while he was disguised in human form.

Popularity: top 1000 →

Edna

Origin: Hebrew meaning "pleasure."

Significance: Sarah's mother in the Book of Tobit.

Popularity: endangered ↓

Judith

Origin: Hebrew meaning "Jewess."

Significance: to encourage her fellow Israelites to have faith that they would vanquish their enemies, Judith won the trust of an enemy general, beheaded him, and took his head back to her people.

Popularity: top 1000 ↓

Related names:

Judy – diminutive – uncommon →

Yudith – Spanish – endangered →

Cross-reference: Because Judith is also the name of a wife of Esau, the name is listed again in the first section of this chapter, "Genesis and Job" (page 9).

Lilith

Origin: Hebrew meaning "of the night."

Significance: a female demon who, according to Jewish tradition, was Adam's first wife, but she was banished from the Garden of Eden.

Popularity: top 1000 ↑

Rafaela

Origin: feminine of Rafael, Hebrew meaning "God heals."

Significance: Rafael is a central figure in the Book of Tobit, in which he helps Tobit, Tobias, and Sarah.

Popularity: endangered →

Sarah

Origin: Hebrew meaning "princess."

Significance: in the Book of Tobit, Sarah is a woman beset by a demon. She had been married seven times, but each time the demon had killed her husband on the wedding night. Tobias

at last drove the demon away and married Sarah himself.

Popularity: top 100 ↓

Cross-reference: Sarah, the wife of Abraham, is a more prominent Biblical figure and is listed in the first section of this chapter, "Genesis and Job" (page 11).

Susan

Origin: short form of Susanna, Hebrew meaning "lily."

Significance: in Catholic and Eastern Orthodox versions of the Book of Daniel, Susanna is blackmailed by two peeping Toms who falsely accuse her of immodest behavior. Daniel comes to her rescue, and the blackmailers are put to death.

Popularity: top 1000 ↓

Related names:

Susanna – Old Testament form – uncommon →

Shoshana – Hebrew – uncommon →

Suzanne – another short form of Susanna – endangered ↓

Susie – diminutive – endangered →

Suzette – diminutive – endangered →

Cross-reference: Another woman named Susanna was a supporter of Jesus. See chapter 2 (page 28).

Toby

Origin: nickname for Tobias, Hebrew meaning "God is good."

Significance: with the help of the angel Raphael, Tobias cured his father of blindness. He also drove away a demon that had plagued a woman named Sarah, whom he then married.

Popularity: ♂ endangered →

Hebrew and Yiddish Names

Many Biblical names are Hebrew in origin. There are, however, Hebrew names aren't in the Bible at all. The non-Biblical names used by Christians, and the few Yiddish names in general use, are included in this section.

Adara

Origin: feminine of Adar, Hebrew meaning "strength."

Popularity: endangered →

Aliza

Origin: Hebrew meaning "joyful."

Popularity: top 1000 →

Related names:

Alize – endangered ↓

Alona

Origin: Hebrew meaning "oak tree."

Popularity: endangered →

Ari

Origin: Hebrew meaning "lion."

Popularity: ♂ uncommon ↑

Eliana

Origin: Hebrew meaning "my God has answered."

Popularity: top 500 ↑

Kayla

Origin: variant spelling of Kaila, Yiddish meaning "laurel" or "crown."

Popularity: top 500 ↓

Spelling variations: *Keyla*

Cross-reference: As a short form of Makayla, Kayla is also listed in earlier in this chapter (page 18) and in "Christian Concepts" in chapter 3 (page 52).

Samara

Origin: Hebrew meaning "protected by God."

Popularity: top 1000 ↓

Selah

Origin: in Psalms, Selah indicates a pause, a time to think about what has been said.

Popularity: top 1000 ↑

Sharon

Origin: the name of a large valley plain on the north coast of Israel. It is Hebrew meaning "forest."

Popularity: top 1000 ↓

Shayna

Origin: Yiddish meaning "beautiful."

Popularity: uncommon ↓

Talia

Origin: Hebrew meaning "dew from God."

Popularity: top 500 ↑

Spelling variations: *Taliyah*

Ziva

Origin: Hebrew meaning "brilliance, splendor."

Popularity: uncommon ↑

Chapter 2: The New Testament

People and Places in the Life of Jesus

New Testament names are surprisingly diverse. They vary in style from classic to old-fashioned and from trendy to off-beat. Some have been popular for so long and in so many countries that they've given rise to dozens of variations. The most prolific names—Mary, John, Elizabeth, and Anne—are grouped into separate sections later in this chapter. These groups of names are fun to read through, and they're a great resource for parents who are looking for an updated version of a family name.

Abilene

Origin: a region in modern-day Syria.

Significance: to establish a time when John the Baptist was preaching baptism and repentance, the Gospel of Luke mentions that a man named Lysanias was the ruler of Abilene.

Popularity: endangered →

Andrea

Origin: short form of Andreas, Greek meaning "manly." In some languages it's masculine, in others feminine—in English it's feminine.

Significance: Andreas is an older form of Andrew, one of the Twelve Apostles.

Popularity: top 500 ↓

Related names:

Andi – diminutive of Andrew and Andrea. Traditionally *Andy* has been a boys' name, and with that spelling it is a top-500 name for boys. The spelling *Andi* is used for girls. – ♂ uncommon ↑

Andriana – another feminine of Andreas – endangered ↓

Drea – short form of Andrea – endangered →

Andrew – English masculine of Andreas – ♂ endangered ↓

Drew – short form of Andrew – ♂ uncommon →

Anderson – a last name meaning "Anders' son"; Anders is a Scandinavian form of Andreas – ♂ endangered ↑

Belen

Origin: Spanish for Bethlehem, a town in Palestine.

Significance: Jesus was born in Bethlehem.

Popularity: top 1000 →

Bethany

Origin: the name of a village near Jerusalem.

Significance: Jesus resurrected Lazarus in Bethany.

Popularity: top 500 ↓

Brielle

Origin: short form of Gabrielle, feminine of Gabriel, Hebrew meaning "God is my strength."

Significance: see Gabriella.

Popularity: top 500 ↑

Related names:

Briella – top 1000 ↑

Cross-reference: Because the angel Gabriel also appears to Daniel, this name is included in chapter 1, "The Old Testament" (page 17).

Candice

Origin: the name of a woman who was once queen of the Ethiopians.

Significance: mentioned in the New Testament because Philip baptized one of Candice's subjects.

Popularity: uncommon ↓

Related names:

Dacey – English diminutive – endangered ↓

Chloe

Origin: Greek meaning "green shoot," a reference to a newly sprouted plant.

Significance: a woman who had a Christian household. Members of her house reported that Christians were arguing about which of the early Church leaders to follow.

Popularity: top 100 ↓

Spelling variations: *Khloe*

Damaris

Origin: Greek, possibly meaning "dominant."

Significance: converted to Christianity by Paul. Her high social position and practical help in organizing the Church made her an important convert.

Popularity: uncommon ↓

Emmanuelle

Origin: used in several Romance languages. It is the name of the Messiah, prophesized in the Book of Isaiah and specified as Mary's child in the Gospel of Matthew.

Significance: a title for Jesus.

Popularity: endangered ↑

Related names:

Emmanuella – endangered ↑

Manuela – endangered →

Eunice

Origin: Greek meaning "good victory."

Significance: the mother of Timothy, a friend of the apostle Paul to whom Paul wrote two epistles that are part of the New Testament. Timothy also worked with Paul on several Biblical texts.

Popularity: uncommon →

Gabriella

Origin: feminine of Gabriel, Hebrew meaning "God is my strength."

Significance: the name of the angel who appeared to Mary to tell her that she would conceive Jesus (Luke 1:26).

Popularity: top 100 ↓

Related names:

Gabrielle – top 500 ↓

Gabby – endangered →

Spelling variations: *Gabriela*

Cross-reference: Because Gabriel also appears to the prophet Daniel, this name is included in chapter 1, "The Old Testament" (page 18).

Galilea (gal-uh-LEE-uh)

Origin: Galilee is a region in modern-day Israel.

Significance: the place where Jesus lived for most of his life and where he ministered to the people.

Popularity: top 1000 →

Gemma

Origin: feminine of the Old French name Gemmes, the origin of English James, Hebrew meaning "supplanter." It derived like this: Hebrew Ya'aqob > Greek Iakobos > Latin Jacobus > Late Latin Jacomus > Old French Gemmes.

Significance: there are two apostles named James: James the brother of Jesus; and James the son of Zebedee and Salome, who was also the brother of the apostle John.

Popularity: top 500 ↑

Jacqueline

Origin: feminine of Jacques, a French form of James. It derived from Hebrew like this: Hebrew Ya'aqob > Greek Iakobos > Latin Jacobus > French Jacques.

Significance: see Gemma.

Popularity: top 500 ↓

Related names:

Jackie – ♂♀ uncommon →

Jamie

Origin: diminutive of James.

Significance: see Gemma.

Popularity: ♂♀ top 500 ↓

Related names:

Jamison – a last name meaning "James' son" – ♂ endangered →

Joanna

Origin: late Latin form of Ioanna, the feminine of Ioannes, which is the Biblical Greek form of John.

Significance: a woman who was healed by Jesus and became a disciple. She was witness to the resurrection.

Popularity: top 500 ↓

Related names:

Joanne – uncommon ↓

Spelling variations: *Johanna*

Cross-reference: Because Joanna is a feminine form of John, it is also listed later in this chapter, in the section on John-names (page 41).

Jordyn

Origin: from the Jordan River, which has its source in Lebanon and flows into the Dead Sea. The name comes from Hebrew *yarden*, "to descend."

Significance: the river in which John the Baptist baptized Jesus.

Popularity: The spellings *Jordyn* and *Jordynn* are far more popular for girls, and *Jordan* is far more popular for boys. ♂♀ top 500 →

Related names:

Jordana – endangered →

Spelling variations: *Jordan, Jordynn*

Josephine

Origin: French feminine of Joseph, Hebrew meaning "God will add," implying the addition of children to a family.

Significance: Joseph married Mary, the mother of Jesus.

Popularity: top 500 ↑

Related names:

Josie – top 500 ↑

Josette – endangered →

Josefina – endangered ↓

Joey – ♂ uncommon →

Jodi – ♂♀ endangered →

Jude

Origin: short form of Judah, Hebrew meaning "to praise."

Significance: a brother of Jesus. Also, Judas Thaddeus was one of the Twelve Apostles and the author of the Epistle of Jude.

Popularity: ♂ uncommon ↑

Junia

Origin: both the name of an ancient Roman family and its feminine form.

Significance: a woman named Junia is mentioned in Romans as a prominent and early apostle of Jesus.

Popularity: endangered ↑

Lois

Origin: possibly Greek meaning "desirable," with a connotation of being good or agreeable.

Significance: Timothy's grandmother. See Eunice.

Popularity: endangered →

Luca

Origin: form of Luke used in many Romance and Slavic languages. It is Latin meaning "man from Lucania," an ancient Italian city.

Significance: Luke the Evangelist was one of the four authors of the Gospels.

Popularity: ♂ endangered →

Lydia

Origin: the name of a rich kingdom in ancient Greece (now in Turkey).

Significance: Lydia was the first Christian convert to be named in the Bible (Acts 16:14-15).

Popularity: top 100 ↑

Maci

Origin: sometimes a short form of Massius, a Roman variation of Matthew, Hebrew meaning "gift of God."

Significance: see Mattie.

Popularity: top 500 ↓

Spelling variations: *Macy, Macie, Macey*

Madeline

Origin: French variation of Magdalene, Greek meaning "from Magdala."

Significance: see Magdalena.

Popularity: top 100 ↓

Related names:

Maddie – nickname for Matthew, Madison, and forms of Madeline – uncommon ↑

Spelling variations: *Madeleine*

Madelyn

Origin: English variation of Madeline.

Significance: see Magdalena.

Popularity: top 100 ↑

Related names:

Maddie – nickname for Matthew, Madison, and forms of Madeline – uncommon ↑

Spelling variations: *Madilyn, Madelynn, Madilynn, Madalyn, Madalynn*

Madison

Origin: blend of "Maddie's son." In this case, Maddie is a nickname for Matthew, Hebrew meaning "gift of God."

Significance: see Mattie.

Popularity: top 10 ↓

Related names:

Maddie – nickname for Matthew, Madison, and forms of Madeline – uncommon ↑

Spelling variations: *Maddison, Madisyn, Madyson*

Magali

Origin: Spanish contraction of Mary Magdalene.

Popularity: endangered ↓

Magdalena

Origin: Latin form of Magdalene, Greek meaning "from Magdala." Mary Magdalene was from Magdala, a fishing village on the Sea of Galilee.

Significance: Mary Magdalene was a follower of Jesus and witness to both the crucifixion and the resurrection.

Popularity: top 1000 →

Related names:

Magdalene – uncommon →

Magda – endangered ↓

Malin

Origin: Scandinavian contraction of Magdalene.

Significance: see Magdalena.

Popularity: endangered →

Marlene

Origin: German contraction of Maria Magdalene.

Significance: see Magdalena.

Popularity: uncommon ↓

Related names:

Marlena – endangered →

Marla – endangered →

Marlen – endangered ↓

Martha

Origin: Aramaic meaning "mistress, lady."

Significance: the sister of Lazarus, who was resurrected by Jesus in the town of Bethany.

Popularity: top 1000 ↓

Mattie

Origin: diminutive of Matthew, Hebrew meaning "gift of God."

Significance: Matthew was one of the Twelve Apostles and one of the four authors of the Gospels.

Popularity: top 1000 ↑

Related names:

Mattea – feminine of Matteo, used in several Romance languages – endangered ↓

Paula

Origin: feminine of Paul, Latin meaning "small."

Significance: Paul preached the gospel to the Gentiles and helped to establish and strengthen new churches. He is also the author of fourteen epistles that form part of the New Testament.

Popularity: top 1000 ↓

Related names:

Paola – used in several Romance languages – top 1000 ↓

Paulina – top 1000 ↓

Pauline – endangered →

Paulette – endangered →

Payson

Origin: an English last name meaning "Paw's son."

Significance: Paw may be a diminutive of Paul.

Popularity: ♂♀ endangered ↓

Petra

Origin: feminine of Petro, the Greek form of Peter, meaning "stone, rock."

Significance: Peter was one of the Twelve Apostles and an important leader of the early Church. He is regarded by Catholics as the first pope.

Popularity: uncommon →

Philippa

Origin: feminine of Philip, Greek meaning "horse-loving."

Significance: Phillip was one of the Twelve Apostles.

Popularity: endangered ↑

Related names:

Pippa – uncommon ↑

Phoebe

Origin: Greek meaning "bright."

Significance: an early church leader and a friend of the apostle Paul.

Popularity: top 500 ↑

Pierce

Origin: from Pierres, an Old French form of Peter, Greek meaning "stone, rock."

Significance: see Petra.

Popularity: ♂ endangered →

Priscilla

Origin: feminine diminutive of Prisca, a Roman family name meaning "ancient."

Significance: Priscilla and her husband Aquila were early disciples and missionaries who are mentioned several times in the New Testament.

Popularity: top 500 ↓

Related names:

Prisca – original form of Priscilla; used in Romans and Timothy – endangered →

Rhoda

Origin: Greek meaning "rose."

Significance: the mother of John Mark, who is also thought to be Mark the Evangelist.

Popularity: endangered →

Salome (sal-O-mee)

Origin: Hebrew meaning "peace."

Significance: a follower of Jesus and the mother of the apostles James and John.

Popularity: uncommon →

Semaj

Origin: James spelled backward.

Significance: see Gemma.

Popularity: ♂ endangered ↓

Simone (see-MONE)

Origin: French feminine of Simon, Hebrew meaning "He has heard."

Significance: another name of the apostle Peter and the name of one of Jesus's brothers.

Popularity: top 1000 ↓

Related names:

Simona (see-MONE-a) – Italian and Slavic – endangered →

Susan

Origin: short form of Susanna, Hebrew meaning "lily."

Significance: mentioned as a woman who helped support Jesus and his disciples (Luke 8:3).

Popularity: top 1000 ↓

Related names:

Susanna – Old Testament form – uncommon →

Shoshana – Hebrew – uncommon →

Suzanne – another short form of Susanna – endangered ↓

Susie – English diminutive – endangered →

Suzette – diminutive – endangered →

Cross-reference: Susanna is also a figure in Catholic and Eastern Orthodox versions of the Book of Daniel. See the section titled, "Old Testament Traditions" in chapter 1 for more information (page 20).

Tabitha

Origin: Aramaic meaning "gazelle.

Significance: an old, charitable woman who was resurrected by Peter.

Popularity: top 1000 ↓

Related names:

Dorcas – Greek meaning "gazelle." Dorcas is used in some Biblical texts in place of Tabitha – endangered →

Tommie

Origin: diminutive of Thomas, Aramaic meaning "twin."

Significance: Thomas was one of the Twelve Apostles, and the only one who doubted Jesus's resurrection.

Popularity: endangered ↓

Ximena (hee-MAYN-a)

Origin: Spanish feminine of Simon, Hebrew meaning "He has heard."

Significance: see Simone.

Popularity: top 500 ↑

Spelling variations: *Jimena*

Mary

The Mary-names, of which there are more than 200, are divided into three groups:

1. Mary and her variations, such as nicknames and non-English forms
2. Mary names from the Catholic tradition, notably Spanish titles, but also French and Italian names, all of which recall miracles, prayers, and churches that honor the Virgin
3. Combination Mary names, like Mariana and Rosemary

Mary and Her Variations

In the Old Testament, Miryam is the name of Moses's big sister, and it was an ultra-popular baby name a little more than 2000 years ago. That's why there are at least six women in the New Testament named Mary, translated into Biblical Greek both as Mariam and Maria. Coincidentally, Maria is also an ancient Roman family name and its feminine form, which may explain why that form became the favorite in Italy and neighboring Spain.

Maria was shortened to Marie in France and carried off to England with the conquering Normans (in 1066). As she travelled through the British Isles, Marie took on more forms than any other girls' name. Those forms came to America, first with the British colonists and later with the great influx of immigrants from Ireland.

The many American Mary-names that come from the British Isles make up only a part of our Mary-story. Names in the US are also strongly influenced by neighboring Latin America and our own large Latino population, so we also use several Spanish, Basque, and Catalan variations of Mary.

Etta

Origin: short form of various names ending with *-etta*, such as Marietta, an Italian diminutive of Maria.

Popularity: uncommon ↑

Related names:

Marietta – endangered →

Maia

Origin: Basque form of Maria.

Popularity: top 1000 →

Maire (MY-rah)

Origin: Irish Gaelic form of Marie.

Popularity: endangered →

Related names:

Maura – (MORE-uh) English form of Maire – uncommon ↓

Mamie (MAY-mee)

Origin: a nickname for Mary. It may have originated as a child's pronunciation—the sound of *r* is notoriously difficult for toddlers to say.

Popularity: endangered →

Maria

Origin: Mariam and Maria are New Testament Greek forms of the Hebrew name Miryam.

Popularity: top 500 ↓

Related names:

Ria – German and Dutch short form – uncommon ↓

Demaria – child of Maria – endangered →

Mari – Basque short form – endangered ↓

Mariah (muh-RYE-uh)

Origin: Until the early 20ᵗʰ century when Spanish and Italian muh-REE-uh became more popular, the usual English pronunciation of *Maria* was muh-RYE-uh. *Mariah* is a new way of spelling this traditional pronunciation.

Popularity: top 500 ↓

Spelling variations: *Mariyah, Moriah*

Marian

Origin: variation of Marion, a French diminutive of Marie.

Popularity: uncommon →

Related names:

Marion – also used as a boys' name, in which case it may be related to the name Marius, the masculine form of the ancient Roman family name Maria – ♂♀ uncommon →

Marie

Origin: French short form of Maria.

Popularity: top 1000 →

Related names:

Marielle – a French diminutive of Marie – endangered →

Mariela

Origin: Italian diminutive of Maria.

Popularity: uncommon ↓

Related names:

Mariel – endangered ↓

Marilyn

Origin: English diminutive of Mary.

Popularity: top 500 ↑

Mariona

Origin: Catalan diminutive of Maria.

Popularity: endangered →

Related names:

Ona – short form – endangered →

Marita

Origin: Germanic diminutive of Maria.

Popularity: endangered →

Related names:

Mitzi – endangered ↓

Mary

Origin: the English form of Marie.

Popularity: top 500 ↓

Related names:

May – contraction of Mary and Margaret – uncommon ↑

Arie – short form of Mary and Carrie – endangered ↑

Cross-reference: May is also listed in chapter 4, "Early Martyrs" (page 74)

Maša (MAH-shah)

Origin: in some Slavic languages, Maša is a transcription of the Russian name Masha, a diminutive of Russian Mariya.

Popularity: endangered →

Mayrin (MORE-een)

Origin: a diminutive of Irish Maire, traditionally spelled *Mairin*.

Popularity: endangered →

Related names:

Maureen – English spelling of Mairin – endangered ↓

Mia

Origin: Germanic contraction of Maria.

Popularity: top 10 ↑

Mimi

Origin: an Italian diminutive of Maria.

Popularity: endangered ↓

Miriam

Origin: variant spelling of Miryam, the older, Hebrew form of Maria.

Popularity: top 500 →

Spelling variations: *Mariam, Maryam*

Cross-reference: Miriam was also the name of Moses's sister and is listed in the section titled "Exodus and Early Years in Canaan" in chapter 1, "The Old Testament" (page 12).

Moira (MOY-ra)

Origin: Gaelic form of Marie. It is more common in Scotland than Ireland.

Popularity: uncommon →

Molly

Origin: variation of Mary, from the old nickname Mally.

Popularity: top 500 ↓

Spelling variations: *Mollie*

Polly

Origin: nickname for Molly. In England, rhyming was once a popular way to create nicknames: Peggy was created the same way from Meggy.

Popularity: endangered →

Mary Names from the Catholic Tradition

This section includes names that come from titles for the Virgin Mary, miracles that are attributed to her, prayers that said in her honor, and churches that were named after her. Some names even come from scriptural commentary about Mary. Specifically, several names come from commentary written by St. Jerome, which is retold in the following "Story of Stella Maris." The names in this section are predominantly Spanish, though some come from French and Italian.

The Story of Stella Maris

1 Kings tells the story of a drought sent by God to Israel to punish the people for worshipping Canaanite gods. Despite three years of drought, the people did not stop worshipping the false gods, so God revealed his power through Elijah. The prophet performed miracles and made the people believe; and at last they repented.

Sitting atop Mount Carmel, Elijah, prayed for an end to the drought—God having granted him that right. He then told his servant to go and look at the sea. The man returned, reporting that there was nothing to be seen. Seven times Elijah sent him back, until at last the servant reported that a small cloud, the size of a man's hand, was floating above the sea. This cloud was the first sign of a heavy rain that would mark the end of the drought.

St. Jerome, writing in the 4th and 5th centuries, compared Mary to this cloud, as both brought relief and forgiveness to the people. In his comparison, he called Mary *stilla maris*, meaning "drop of the sea" in Latin. An error in copying sometime later changed this to *stella maris*, meaning "star of the sea," which is also a name for the North Star. St. Jerome's text was gradually reinterpreted as comparing Mary to that heavenly star that guides travelers along the right path.

Araceli

Origin: from one of two churches: Santa Maria in Aracoeli (meaning "altar of Heaven"), a prestigious church located at the top of one of Rome's seven hills; or Santa Maria in Araceli, a 13th century Italian church in Vicenza, Italy.

Popularity: uncommon ↓

Carmen

Origin: a Spanish name, taken from the title *Virgen del Carmen*, "Virgin of Carmel," arising from devotions to the Virgin by the monks of the Carmelite order. The Carmelites were hermits who lived on Mount Carmel. See "The Story of Stella Maris" above.

Popularity: top 500 ↓

Related names:

Carmella – uncommon ↑

Carmel – ♂♀ endangered →

Carmelita – endangered →

Concetta

Origin: Italian meaning "conception," from the title *Maria Concetta*, which recalls the Immaculate Conception.

Popularity: endangered →

Related names:

Etta – short form of names ending with *–etta* – uncommon ↑

Concepción – Spanish equivalent of Concetta, from *Maria Concepción* – endangered ↓

Consuelo

Origin: a Spanish name, taken from the title *Nuestra Señora del Consuelo*, "Our Lady of Consolation."

Popularity: endangered ↓

Estrella

Origin: from *Estrella de Mar*, the Spanish form of *Stella Maris*. See "The Story of Stella Maris" on the previous page.

Popularity: top 1000 ↓

Guadalupe

Origin: a province in Mexico where the Virgin is said to have appeared.

Popularity: top 500 ↓

Related names:

Lupita – nickname – uncommon ↓

Lola

Origin: nickname for Dolores, which is a Spanish name that comes from *María de los Dolores*, for a set of Catholic prayers, called "The Seven Sorrows of Mary" in English.

Popularity: top 500 →

Related names:

Dolores – endangered →

Lourdes (LUR-dess)

Origin: Lourdes is a town in France where a fourteen-year-old shepherdess named Bernadette had multiple visions of the Virgin.

Popularity: endangered ↓

Cross-reference: Bernadette is listed separately in chapter 5 in the section titled "Later Saints" (page 91).

Luz

Origin: a Spanish name, taken from the title *Nuestra Señora de la Luz*, "Our Lady of Light."

Popularity: uncommon ↓

Related names:

Mariluz – endangered →

Madonna

Origin: Italian meaning "my lady," a title of respect for the Virgin.

Popularity: endangered →

Related names:

Donna – uncommon ↓

Marisol

Origin: Spanish contraction of the title *María de la Soledad*, "Our Lady of Solitude."

Popularity top 1000 ↓

Related names:

Soledad – endangered ↓

Marissa

Origin: from *Stella Maris*. For more information, read "The Story of Stella Maris" at the beginning of this section.

Popularity: top 500 ↓

Related names:

Maritza – uncommon ↓

Maris – endangered →

Mercedes

Origin: a Spanish name, taken from the title *Santa María de las Mercedes*, "Saint Mary of Mercies."

Popularity: top 1000 ↓

Milagros

Origin: a Spanish name, taken from the title *Nuestra Señora de los Milagros*, "Our Lady of Miracles."

Popularity: uncommon ↓

Related names:

Milagro – endangered →

Paz

Origin: a Spanish name, taken from the title *Nuestra Señora de la Paz*, "Our Lady of Peace."

Popularity: endangered →

Pilar

Origin: a Spanish name, taken from the title *Nuestra Señora del Pilar*, "Our Lady of the Pillar." This title recalls Saint James' vision of Mary on a pillar being carried angels.

Popularity: endangered →

Rocio

Origin: a Spanish name, taken from *María del Rocío*, "Mary of the Dew," for a famous statue of the mother and child that stands in the Hermitage of El Rocio, in Spain.

Popularity: endangered ↓

Rosario

Origin: a Spanish name, taken from the title *Nuestra Señora del Rosario*, "Our Lady of the Rosary."

Popularity: endangered ↓

Stella

Origin: from *Stella Maris*. For more information, read "The Story of Stella Maris" at the beginning of this section.

Popularity: top 100 ↑

Related names:

Stellarose – endangered ↑

Mary Combination Names

Individually, only a few of the combination Mary-names are really popular: Mariana, Marilyn, and Rosemary, for example. However, they are worth considering for a couple of reasons. To begin with, many of these names have an old-fashioned appeal that is currently quite popular. Names like Maryellen and Maryjane fit right in with the style of vintage favorites such as Charlotte and Alice.

It's also interesting to look at the combination names as a group. Even though most are given to only a handful of babies each year, as a group the Mary-combinations were given to more than 4,000 girls in 2014.

Adamary

Origin: combination of Ada + Mary. Ada is a Germanic name with no special Christian significance.

Popularity: endangered ↓

Avamarie

Origin: combination of Ava + Marie. Ava is a Germanic name with no special Christian significance.

Popularity: endangered ↑

Dulcemaria

Origin: Spanish meaning "sweet Maria." It is a combination of Dulce + Maria.

Popularity: endangered →

Ellamarie

Origin: combination of Ella + Marie. Ella is a short form of names ending with -*ella*, like Gabriella.

Popularity: endangered →

Related names:

  Maryella – endangered ↑

Evamarie

Origin: combination of Eva + Marie. Eva is a form of the Old Testament name Eve.

Popularity: endangered →

Jasmarie

Origin: combination of Jasmine + Marie. Jasmine is the name of a fragrant flower with no special Christian significance.

Popularity: endangered →

Maite (my-TEH)

Origin: Basque contraction of Maria Esther or Maria Teresa.

Popularity: uncommon →

Cross-reference: Maite is also listed with the Old Testament names (page 18) and with the saints' names (page 92).

Mariafernanda

Origin: combination of Maria + Fernanda. Fernanda is a feminine of Ferdinand, the name of a medieval Castilian saint and king.

Popularity: endangered →

Related names:

  Marifer – endangered →

Maribel

Origin: contraction of Mariaisabel. Isabel is a variation of Elizabeth, the mother of John the Baptist.

Popularity: uncommon ↓

Related names:

Marybelle – endangered →

Maribella – endangered ↓

Marisabel – endangered ↓

Mariaisabel – endangered →

Maryelizabeth – endangered →

Marybeth – endangered ↓

Isabellamarie – endangered →

Lisamarie – endangered →

Mariana

Origin: combination of Mary + Anna. See the Anne-names later in this chapter for information about Anna (page 45).

Popularity: top 500 ↓

Related names:

Maryann – uncommon ↓

Annamarie – uncommon ↓

Annmarie – uncommon ↓

Spelling variations: *Marianna*

Mariangel

Origin: combination of Maria + Angel. An angel is a heavenly being whom God sends to bear messages or to help people.

Popularity: endangered →

Maricruz

Origin: combination of Maria + Cruz. *Cruz* is Spanish meaning "cross."

Popularity: endangered ↓

Marilyn

Origin: English diminutive of Mary, but it is often taken as a combination of the names Mary + Lynn. Lynn is a Welsh name with no special Christian significance.

Popularity: top 500 ↑

Maryalice

Origin: combination of Mary + Alice. Alice is a variation of Adelaide, the name of a medieval saint.

Popularity: endangered →

Maryclaire

Origin: combination of Mary + Claire. Claire is the name of a medieval Italian saint.

Popularity: endangered →

Maryellen

Origin: combination of Mary + Ellen. Ellen is a variation of Helen, the name of an early martyr.

Popularity: endangered →

Related names:

Mariaelena – endangered ↓

Marielena – endangered ↓

Marygrace

Origin: combination of Mary + Grace. Grace is a reference to the kindness shown by God to mankind.

Popularity: endangered →

Maryjane

Origin: combination of Mary + Jane. Jane is a feminine of John.

Popularity: uncommon ↓

Marykate

Origin: combination of Mary + Kate. Kate is a short form of Katherine, the name of an early martyr.

Popularity: endangered ↓

Related names:

Marykatherine – endangered ↓

Marymargaret

Origin: combination of Mary + Margaret, an early martyr.

Popularity: endangered →

Rosemary

Origin: combination of Rose + Mary. Rose is typically used as a flower name, although there is a 17th century Peruvian saint by that name.

Popularity: endangered ↑

Related names:

Romy – German contraction of Rosemarie – endangered →

Rosamaria – endangered ↓

Maryrose – endangered ↑

Sophiamarie

Origin: combination of Sophia + Marie. Sophia is the name of an early martyr.

Popularity: endangered →

Christmas

Adora

Origin: short form of the Spanish name Adoración.

Significance: a reference to the Adoration of the Magi, when the three Magi gave their gifts to the baby Jesus.

Popularity: endangered →

Belen

Origin: Spanish for Bethlehem, a town in Palestine.

Significance: Jesus was born in Bethlehem.

Popularity: top 1000 →

Brielle

Origin: short form of Gabrielle, feminine of Gabriel, Hebrew meaning "God is my strength."

Significance: see Gabriella.

Popularity: top 500 ↑

Related names:

Briella – top 1000 ↑

Cross-reference: Brielle is also listed in chapter 1 (page 17).

Carol

Origin: feminine of Carl, Germanic meaning "man," with the connotation "common man" or "freeman." Coincidentally, *carol* is also Old French for a kind of round dance that was accompanied by joyful singing.

Significance: Carol is the common English word for a Christmas song.

Popularity: uncommon ↓

Cross-reference: Carol is also listed in chapter 5 "Saints" (page 84).

Emmanuelle

Origin: feminine of Emmanuel, Hebrew meaning "God is with us."

Significance: Emmanuel is the name of the Messiah, prophesized in the Book of Isaiah and specified as Mary's child in the Gospel of Matthew.

Popularity: endangered ↑

Related names:

Emmanuella – endangered ↑

Manuela – endangered →

Gabriella

Origin: feminine of Gabriel, Hebrew meaning "God is my strength."

Significance: Gabriel is the name of the angel who appeared to Mary to tell her that she would conceive Jesus.

Popularity: top 100 ↓

Related names:

Gabrielle – top 500 ↓

Gabby – endangered →

Spelling variations: *Gabriela*

Cross-reference: Because Gabriel also appears to the prophet Daniel, this name is included in chapter 1, "The Old Testament" in the section titled "The Israelites in Exile" (page 18).

Holly

Origin: Old English word for an evergreen bush with sharply pointed leaves and bright red berries. It comes from an older word meaning "to prick."

Significance: holly is a pretty green and red bush that is a symbol of Christmas time.

Popularity: top 500 ↓

Related names:

Hollis – plural, for holly bushes – traditionally a boys' name, but now almost as common for girls. – ♂♀ uncommon ↑

Messiah

Origin: Hebrew meaning "anointed," used for a leader who has saved/freed his people.

Significance: a title for Jesus.

Popularity: ♂ endangered ↓

Natalia

Origin: from Latin *natalis dies*, meaning "birthday."

Significance: a reference to Christmas, the day Jesus was born.

Popularity: top 500 →

Related names:

Natasha – Russian nickname – top 1000 ↓

Spelling variations: *Natalya*

Natalie

Origin: short form of Natalia.

Significance: see Natalia.

Popularity: top 100 ↓

Spelling variations: *Nathalie, Nataly, Nathaly, Natalee*

Noelle

Origin: feminine of Noel, a French variation of Latin *natalis dies*, meaning "birthday."

Significance: a reference to Christmas, the day Jesus was born.

Popularity: top 500 ↑

Related names:

Noella – French – uncommon ↑

Noelia – Spanish – endangered ↓

Tiffany

Origin: from the Greek for "epiphany," meaning "manifestation."

Significance: Epiphany is a holiday that falls on January 6 and marks the day on which the Magi visited the baby Jesus, and therefore the day on which he was revealed to the Gentiles.

Popularity: top 500 ↓

Related names:

Epiphany – endangered →

John

Of all the names used in America, not one has more variations than John. The girls' names alone number more than three dozen, from Asia to Zaneta. John was one of the first Biblical names used in England, in the medieval French form Jehan. The name spread throughout the British Isles, where each country developed its own spelling, pronunciation, and nicknames, most of which came to America with early colonists or later immigrants. In addition to many British variations, the US has feminine forms of John from Italy, Spain, Germany, Poland, and Russia.

John was the name of two men who were very close to Jesus: his cousin, John the Baptist, and the apostle John, who is believed to have written five of the books in the New Testament. The Hebrew form Yohanan, meaning "He has favored," was transliterated into New Testament Greek as Ioannes and became Iouavannes in Late Latin, the source of *v*-variations like Evan, Ivan, and Giovanni.

Asia (AH-shah)

Origin: short form of Joasia, a Polish nickname for Johanna.

Popularity: top 1000 ↓

Evan

Origin: Welsh form of John.

Popularity: ♂ endangered →

Gianna

Origin: contraction of Giovanna.

Popularity: top 100 ↓

Related names:

Gia – top 500 →

Gianella – endangered →

Giabella – endangered →

Gionna – endangered →

Gianni – ♂ endangered →

Spelling variations: *Giana*

Giovanna

Origin: feminine of Giovanni, an Italian form of John.

Popularity: top 1000 →

Ivanna

Origin: feminine of Ivan, a Slavic form of John.

Popularity: top 1000 ↑

Related names:

Iva – endangered ↑

Vanna – endangered ↑

Vania – endangered →

Ivanka – endangered →

Jana (JAH-nah)

Origin: feminine of Jan, a Germanic form of John.

Popularity: uncommon →

Related names:

Yana (YAH-nah) – Slavic form of Jana that reflects the German pronunciation – endangered →

Janae (juh-NAY)

Origin: variation of Jane, commonly used in the Mormon community, where it is written JaNae.

Popularity: top 1000 ↓

Jane

Origin: variation of Joan, an English feminine of John.

Popularity: top 500 ↑

Related names:

  Janelle – top 500 →

  Janie – uncommon ↓

  Jayna – uncommon ↓

  Janet – uncommon ↓

  Janella – endangered ↑

  Janelly – endangered →

  Yanet – endangered ↓

Janice

Origin: probably a variation of Jane. It was first used in the novel *Janice Meredith*, an 1899 Revolutionary War romance by Paul Leicester Ford.

Popularity: uncommon ↓

Jeanne (JEEN)

Origin: feminine of Jean, the French form of John.

Popularity: endangered ↓

Related names:

  Jeanette – diminutive of Jeanne – uncommon ↓

  Nettie – diminutive of Jeannette and Annette – endangered →

  Zaneta – Polish variation of Jeanette – endangered →

  Janine – diminutive of Jeanne, traditionally spelled *Jeannine* – endangered ↓

  Janina – variation of Janine – endangered →

  Emmajean – endangered →

Jenna

Origin: variation of Jenny, a medieval English diminutive of Jeanne.

Popularity: top 500 ↓

Related names:

  Jenny – top 1000 ↓

  Jenelle – endangered →

Jensen

Origin: a last name meaning "Jens' son." Jens is a Germanic form of John.

Popularity: ♂ endangered →

Jessie

Origin: Scottish nickname for Jeanne.

Popularity: top 1000 ♂♀ →

Cross-reference: Though Jessie and Jesse are pronounced the same way, the two names are not related: Jesse was the father of King David and is listed in "The Old Testament" (page 16); Jessie is also a nickname for Jessica, an unrelated name coined by Shakespeare.

Joan

Origin: English feminine of John.

Popularity: enormously popular for nearly 1,000 years, Joan's use has been declining steadily since the 1950s, so it is now fairly uncommon for girls. Joán (jo-AHN) is a Catalan form of John/Juan used for boys, and its popularity has been growing. The result is that Joan is now given to twice as many boys as girls. ♂ endangered →

Related names:

Joni – endangered →

Cross-reference: Because Joan of Arc is an important medieval saint, Joan is also listed in chapter 5, "Saints" (page 87).

Joanna

Origin: late Latin form of Ioanna, feminine of Ioannes, the Biblical Greek form of John.

Popularity: top 500 ↓

Related names:

Joanne – uncommon ↓

Spelling variations: *Johanna*

Cross-reference: Joanna is also the name of a woman who was healed by Jesus and became one of his followers. For more information, see the section titled "People and Places in the Life of Jesus," earlier in this chapter (page 24).

Jovanna

Origin: feminine of Jovan, a form of John used in some Romance and some Slavic languages.

Popularity: endangered ↓

Juana

Origin: feminine of Juan, a Spanish form of John.

Popularity: uncommon ↓

Related names:

Juanita – endangered ↓

Navi

Origin: Ivan spelled backward. It's a nickname for the constellation Cassiopeia, given in honor of astronaut Gus Grissom, whose middle name was Ivan, a Slavic form of John.

Popularity: endangered ↑

Siobhan (shih-VAHN)

Origin: Irish feminine of Jehanne, an Old French form of Jean/John.

Popularity: endangered →

Shawna

Origin: feminine of Sean, an Irish form of John. In Ireland it is spelled *Shauna* or *Siana*.

Popularity: endangered ↓

Related names:

Shayne – an English form of Sean – endangered ♂♀ →

Siân (SHAHN) – a Welsh form of Jeanne – endangered ↓

Siani (SHAHN-ee) – a diminutive of Siân – endangered →

Elizabeth

Elisheba is a Hebrew name meaning "God is my oath." In the Old Testament, Elisheba was the wife of Aaron. In the New Testament, the name was transliterated into Greek as Elisabet, who was the mother of John the Baptist.

The much-loved Isabella variation originated in Provence. In some countries, Isabella became more popular than the original Elisabet. This was certainly true in England: King Henry II had two wives, a daughter, and a granddaughter, all named Isabella. (The granddaughter grew up to be Holy Roman empress, adding to the name's popularity.) From about 1300, Isabella was one of the ten most given names in England, with Elisabeth trailing just a bit behind.

The decline of Isabella as an English name began in the 1500s with the reign of Queen Elizabeth I. Her name, and the many affectionate nicknames coined for her, became quintessentially English. Meanwhile, Isabella fell so entirely out of use for so many centuries that it came have a distinctly foreign sound. This remained true, in England and the US, until quite recently. It wasn't until the 1990s that Isabella came back into the American mainstream, rising so quickly in popularity that by 2003 she had become one of the country's most given-names, as she still is.

Bella

Origin: a short form of Isabella.

Popularity: top 100 ↓

Related names:

Belle – uncommon ↑

Belicia – endangered ↓

Cross-reference: Bella is listed twice in chapter 3: with "Short Forms" (page 56) and "Positive Characteristics" (page 60).

Beth

Origin: a short form of Elizabeth.

Popularity: endangered ↓

Related names:

Betty – diminutive of Beth – uncommon ↑

Betsy – English diminutive of Betty, on the same pattern as Patsy from Patty and itsy-bitsy from itty-bitty – uncommon →

Bess – variation of Beth – endangered →

Bessie – diminutive of Bess – endangered →

Bette – short form of Elizabeth – endangered →

Bettina – German diminutive of Elisabeth – endangered ↓

Cross-reference: Beth is also listed in chapter 1 (page 8).

Chevelle

Origin: a variation of Isabel.

Popularity: uncommon ↑

Related names:

Chevy – ♂ endangered ↑

Elizabeth

Origin: English form of Elisabet.

Popularity: top 100 ↓

Related names:

Elsie – diminutive of Elspeth – top 500 ↑

Elspeth – contraction of Elizabeth – endangered →

Spelling variations: *Elisabeth*

Elise

Origin: short form of Elisabeth.

Popularity: top 500 ↑

Related names:

Elsa – top 500 ↑

Elisa – top 500 →

Spelling variations: *Elyse*

Eliza

Origin: short form of Elizabeth.

Popularity: top 500 ↑

Related names:

Liza – uncommon →

Elize – endangered →

Isabella

Origin: elaboration of Isabel.

Popularity: top 10 ↓

Related names:

Izzy – diminutive – ♂♀ endangered ↑

Isa – short form; also an Arabic form of Jesus – ♂♀ endangered →

Sabella – short form – endangered →

Isela – contraction – endangered ↓

Spelling variations: *Izabella, Isabela*

Isabelle

Origin: Provençal variation of Elisabet.

Popularity: top 100 →

Related names:

Isabeau – medieval French form of Isabel – endangered →

Spelling variations: *Isabel*

Libby

Origin: shortened and contracted diminutive of Elizabeth.

Popularity: top 1000 →

Liliana

Origin: elaboration of Lillian.

Popularity: top 500 ↑

Related names:

Lilyann – uncommon ↑

Spelling variations: *Lilliana, Lilyana, Lilianna, Lillianna, Lilyanna*

Lillian

Origin: though often taken as an elaboration of the flower name Lily, Lillian originated as a nickname for Elizabeth.

Popularity: top 100 ↑

Related names:

Lillia – short form – endangered →

Lili – French diminutive of Elisabeth – endangered ↓

Spelling variations: *Lilian*

Lisa

Origin: short form of Elisa.

Popularity: top 1000 ↓

Related names:

Liza – uncommon →

Lizbeth

Origin: shortened and contracted form of Elizabeth.

Popularity: top 1000 ↓

Related names:

Lizeth – uncommon ↓

Lizette – endangered ↓

Liesl – endangered ↑

Lizzie – endangered →

Liz – endangered ↓

Monalisa

Origin: from the famous painting by Leonardo da Vinci. *Monna,* was an old Italian contraction of *madonna,* meaning "my lady." The woman in the painting is probably Lisa Gherardini, hence the title "My Lady Lisa."

Popularity: endangered →

Elizabeth Combination Names

Annalise

Origin: Anna combined with a form of Elizabeth. Anna relates to three Biblical figures. See the following section on Anne-names for information about those three figures (page 45).

Popularity: top 500 ↑

Related names:

Annalisa – uncommon →

Annabeth – uncommon ↑

Lilibeth

Origin: combination of two forms of Elizabeth.

Popularity: endangered ↓

Lilou

Origin: French combination of Lili and Louise. Lili is the French form of Lily, a diminutive of Elizabeth. Louise is a saint's name.

Popularity: endangered ↑

Maryelizabeth

Origin: combination of Mary + Elizabeth.

Popularity: endangered →

Related names:

Marybeth – endangered ↓

Lisamarie – endangered →

Isabellamarie – endangered →

Marisabel – endangered ↓

Sarabeth

Origin: combination of Sara + Beth. In the Old Testament, Sarah is the wife of Abraham.

Popularity: endangered →

Anne

In addition to the familiar English and Spanish forms of Anne, the German variation Annika and several exotic-sounding Slavic forms have become popular in recent years. Ultimately, they all come from the Hebrew name Hannah, which means "God has favored me." This group of names has three Biblical sources:

1. In the Old Testament, Hannah was the mother of Samuel. When she was childless, Hannah prayed for a baby, whom she promised to give back to the service of God, and her prayer was answered.

2. In the New Testament, Anna is the name of an old widow and prophetess who lived at the temple. When Mary and Joseph brought the infant Jesus to the temple, Anna "… talked about the child to everyone who had been waiting expectantly for God to rescue Jerusalem" (Luke 2:36-38).

3. In sources that are accepted by the Catholic and Eastern Orthodox churches (though not by Protestant churches), Anne is the mother of Mary, and therefore the grandmother of Jesus. The Gospel of James is one such source.

Anika

Origin: Germanic diminutive of Anna.

Popularity: top 1000 ↓

Spelling variations: *Annika*

Aniyah

Origin: variation of Anya/Ania.

Popularity: top 500 ↓

Related names:

Anayah – uncommon ↑

Spelling variations: *Aniya*

Anna

Origin: variation of Hannah and an older form of Anne.

Popularity: top 100 ↓

Related names:

Santana – Spanish contraction of Santa Ana (Saint Anne) – ♂ uncommon →

Spelling variations: *Ana*

Anne

Origin: short form of Anna.

Popularity: top 1000 ↓

Related names:

Anita – Spanish diminutive – uncommon ↓

Annette – French diminutive – endangered ↓

Nettie – diminutive of Jeannette and Annette – uncommon →

Spelling variations: *Ann*

Annie

Origin: English diminutive of Anne.

Popularity: top 500 →

Anya

Origin: Slavic diminutive of Anna.

Popularity: top 500 →

Related names:

Anushka – endangered ↓

Spelling variations: *Aanya*

Hannah

Origin: Hebrew meaning "God has graced (favored) me."

Popularity: top 100 ↓

Spelling variations: *Hanna*

Nancy

Origin: originally a nickname for Annis, the medieval pronunciation of Agnes. It was borrowed as a nickname for Anne because Annis and Anne sound so similar.

Popularity: top 1000 ↓

Ann/Anna Combination Names

The most popular endings for American girls' names are *-ann*, *-anna*, and *-ana*. In fact, more than 1000 of the names currently used in the US have one of these endings. Because I don't want to write an *entire* book about the name Anna, I've narrowed it down a bit. This section does not repeat names included in other sections, such as Christiana and Jordana, which are really elaborations of other names. Nor does it include combinations of Ann and Anna with non-Christian names, like Rayann and Aubrianna.

Alexiana

Origin: combination of Alex + Anna. Several names begin with Alex, notably Alexandra, the name of an early martyr; and Alexis, the name of a medieval saint.

Popularity: endangered →

Related names:

Lexianna – endangered →

Aliciana

Origin: combination of Alice or Alicia + Anna. Both are variations of Adelaide, the name of a medieval saint.

Popularity: endangered →

Anasofia

Origin: combination of Anna + Sophia. Sophia is the name of an early martyr.

Popularity: endangered →

Annabelle

Origin: variation of Amabel, a medieval French name meaning "loveable." Amabel comes from Amabilis, the name of two saints, but, Annabelle is often taken as a combination of Anna + Belle.

Popularity: top 100 ↑

Related names:

Annabella – top 500 ↑

Annebelle – endangered ↑

Spelling variations: *Annabel, Annabell*

Annaclaire

Origin: combination of Anna + Claire. Claire is the name of a medieval Italian saint.

Popularity: endangered →

Annagrace

Origin: combination of Anna + Grace. Grace is a reference to the kindness shown by God to mankind.

Popularity: endangered →

Related names:

   Hannahgrace – endangered →

   Graceann – endangered →

Annakate

Origin: combination of Anna + Kate. Kate is a short form of Katherine, the name of an early martyr.

Popularity: endangered →

Annalena

Origin: combination of Anna + Lena. Lena is a short from of names ending with -lena, such as Magdalena and Elena.

Popularity: endangered →

Annalia

Origin: combination of Anna + Lia. Lia is a variant spelling of the Old Testament name Leah.

Popularity: endangered →

Annalise

Origin: Anna combined with a form of Elizabeth.

Popularity: top 500 ↑

Related names:

   Annalisa – uncommon →

   Annabeth – uncommon ↑

Annalucia

Origin: combination of Anna + Lucia. Lucia is the name of an early martyr.

Popularity: endangered →

Annalynn

Origin: combination of Anna + Lynn. Lynn is a Welsh name with no special

Christian significance. However, Annalynn is often seen as a diminutive of Anna, following the pattern of names like Marilyn, Kaitlyn, and Carolyn.

Popularity: endangered ↑

Emiliana

Origin: combination of Emily or Emilia + Anna. Saint Emilia was the mother of five saints, most notably Saint Basil.

Popularity: uncommon ↑

Gabrianna

Origin: combination of Gabrielle + Anna. Gabriel is the name of an angel who appears in both the Old and New Testaments.

Popularity: endangered →

Georgiana

Origin: combination of George + Anna. George is the name of an early martyr.

Popularity: endangered ↑

Gloriana

Origin: combination of Glory + Anna. It was first used in the epic poem *The Faerie Queene*, written by Edmund Spencer during the reign of Queen Elizabeth I. In the poem, Gloriana was the fairy queen, and the name later became a title for Elizabeth.

Popularity: endangered ↑

Hannelore

Origin: German combination of Hanna + Eleonore. Eleonore is a form of Helen, the name of two early saints.

Popularity: endangered →

Mariana

Origin: combination of Mary + Anna.

Popularity: top 500 ↓

Related names:

    Maryann – uncommon ↓

    Annamarie – uncommon ↓

    Annmarie – uncommon ↓

Spelling variations: *Marianna*

Mollyann

Origin: combination of Molly + Ann. Molly is a nickname for Mary.

Popularity: endangered →

Rosanna

Origin: combination of Rose + Anna. Rose is typically used as a flower name, although there is a 17th century Peruvian saint by that name.

Popularity: endangered →

Related names:

    Roseann – endangered →

    Annarose – endangered →

Ruthanne

Origin: combination of Ruth + Anne. Ruth is an Old Testament name.

Popularity: endangered →

Torianna

Origin: combination of Tori + Anna; Tori is a short form of Victoria, the feminine form of Victor, which early Christians used as a reference to Jesus's victory over death.

Popularity: endangered ↓

Chapter 3: Christian Concepts and Virtues

Christian Concepts

Ainsley

Origin: an English last name meaning "meadow of the hermitage."

Significance: Christian hermits tried to live in absolute solitude, dedicating their lives to prayer and worship. The life of a hermit was one of extreme penance on behalf of all Christians.

Popularity: top 500 ↑

Spelling variations: *Ansley*

Amen

Origin: Hebrew meaning "truth" or "so be it."

Significance: the word said at the end of a prayer.

Popularity: ♂♀ endangered ↑

Anastasia

Origin: Greek meaning "resurrection."

Significance: used by early Christians as a reference to the resurrection of Jesus. Its popularity was increased by remembrance of an 3rd century martyr named Anastasia, who was killed on Christmas day.

Popularity: top 500 →

Related names:

Anya – top 500 →

Stacy – uncommon ↓

Cross-reference: Anastasia is also listed in chapter 4 (page 66).

Angel

Origin: Greek meaning "messenger."

Significance: angels are heavenly beings whom God sends to bear messages or to help people.

Popularity: ♂ top 500 ↓

Related names:

Angelique – top 500 →

Angela – top 500 ↓

Angelina – top 500 ↓

Angelica – top 500 ↓

Angeline – top 1000 →

Angie – top 1000 ↓

Angely – uncommon ↑

Angelyn – endangered →

Angelic – endangered →

Angeles – endangered ↓

Angelia – endangered ↓

Angelita – endangered ↓

Aniela – Polish form of Angela – endangered →

Beulah

Origin: Hebrew meaning "married" or "bride."

Significance: in some Christian literature, Beulah is an idyllic land between heaven and earth, found near the end of life's journey. It is used in this sense in John Bunyan's *Pilgrim's Progress*.

Popularity: endangered →

Cross-reference: Beulah is also listed in chapter 1, "The Old Testament," in the section titled "The Kingdom of Israel" (page 15).

Celeste

Origin: both French and Italian meaning "sky, heaven." Forms of the name were used by early Christians.

Significance: see Heaven.

Popularity: top 500 ↓

Related names:

Celestine – Latin – endangered →

Celestina – Spanish and Italian – endangered →

Celestia – English variation – endangered →

Celestial – adjective – endangered ↓

Christabelle

Origin: variation of the Christina names, with the popular *-belle* ending, meaning "beautiful" in French.

Significance: See Christina.

Popularity: endangered →

Related names:

Christabella – endangered →

Christina

Origin: feminine of Christian, from Greek *khristos*, meaning "the anointed." Forms of the name were used by early Christians.

Significance: Christian is the usual English word for a follower of Jesus.

Popularity: top 500 ↓

Related names:

Christine – top 1000 ↓

Christiana – uncommon ↓

Christian – ♂ uncommon ↓

Chrisette – endangered ↑

Chrissy – endangered ↑

Christy – endangered ↓

Spelling variations: *Kristina*

Cielo

Origin: Latin meaning "sky" or "heaven."

Significance: see Heaven.

Popularity: uncommon →

Crosby

Origin: Middle English meaning "cross settlement."

Significance: originally a last name that probably referred to someone who lived near a stone cross erected as a road marker or a memorial.

Popularity: ♂ endangered ↑

Desirée

Origin: French form of Desiderata, a Latin name meaning "to long for."

Significance: Desiderata was used by early Christians to mean they longed for Jesus.

Popularity: top 1000 ↓

Related names:

Desi – short form of Desideria, the Spanish form of Desirée – ♂♀ endangered →

Desire – endangered ↓

Destiny

Origin: Latin, related to "destination" and "determine."

Significance: the idea that the fate of one's life is predetermined.

Popularity: top 500 ↓

Ember

Origin: from Old English *ymbryne*, meaning "around the course."

Significance: Ember is an early Catholic tradition of fasting that is still observed in some countries, though not in the US. There are four Ember weeks, one near the beginning of each season, and for each week there are three Ember days: Wednesday, Friday, and Saturday.

Popularity: top 500 ↑

Eternity

Origin: ultimately from Latin meaning "permanent, enduring."

Significance: in theology, endless life after death.

Popularity: endangered →

Evangeline

Origin: Greek meaning "good news."

Significance: a reference to the Gospel, stories that teach us about Jesus's life.

Popularity: top 500 ↑

Related names:

Evangelina – uncommon →

Grace

Origin: Latin meaning "favor, gratitude."

Significance: the kindness shown by God to mankind.

Popularity: top 100 ↓

Related names:

Gracie – diminutive of Grace – top 500 ↓

Graciela – diminutive of Gracia – uncommon ↓

Gracia – used in several Romance languages – endangered →

Sophiagrace – endangered ↑

Ellagrace – endangered ↑

Emmagrace – endangered ↑

Hannahgrace – endangered →

Annagrace – endangered →

Avagrace – endangered →

Marygrace – endangered →

Graceann – endangered ↓

Gracelyn

Origin: diminutive of Grace.

Significance: see Grace.

Popularity: top 500 ↑

Spelling variations: *Gracelynn*

Hallelujah

Origin: Hebrew meaning "praise Yahweh."

Significance: a joyful exclamation uttered during worship.

Popularity: endangered →

Halo

Origin: Greek meaning "circle of light around the sun or moon."

Significance: a circular glow around the head of person, used in art to indicate that the person is holy.

Popularity: uncommon ↑

Hila – Hebrew form – endangered →

Haven

Origin: Old Norse meaning "harbor, port."

Significance: a place of safety.

Popularity: top 500 ↑

Heaven

Origin: Old English meaning "sky" and later "home of God."

Significance: a holy place above the earth where dwell God, the angels, and the souls of the worthy dead.

Popularity: top 500 →

Related names:

Heavenly – uncommon →

Hosanna

Origin: Aramaic meaning "save, rescue."

Significance: Hosanna is an exclamation of joyful praise.

Popularity: endangered ↑

Jaycee

Origin: blend of the letters *J* and *C*, the initials of Jesus Christ.

Significance: Jesus is the manifestation of God on earth, in human form.

Popularity: top 1000 ↓

Journey

Origin: Old French meaning "day's travel."

Significance: the concept of a journey is often used as a metaphor for Christian life. In centuries past, the use of this name more likely referred to pilgrimages.

Popularity: top 1000 ↑

Kayla

Origin: short form of Makayla, an alternate spelling of Michaela. Michaela is the Germanic feminine of Michael, Hebrew meaning "Who is like God?"

Significance: see Makayla.

Popularity: top 500 ↓

Spelling variations: *Keyla*

Cross-reference: Kayla is also listed twice in chapter 1 (pages 18 and 21).

Kesha

Origin: short form of Vikesha, a Russian form of Vincent, from Latin meaning "conquering."

Significance: Vincentius was a name used by early Christians as a reference to Jesus's victory over death.

Popularity: Traditionally, Kesha is used for boys in Russia, but is used exclusively for girls in the US – endangered →

Kristen

Origin: variation of Christian, from Greek *khristos*, meaning "the anointed." Forms of the name were used by early Christians.

Significance: see Christina.

Popularity: top 1000 ↓

Related names:

Krista – uncommon ↓

Kirsten – uncommon ↓

Kyrie (KEER-ee-aay)

Origin: from *Kyrie eleison*, a pre-Christian, Greek prayer. It means "Lord have mercy."

Significance: Christians traditionally said the prayer during the lighting of lamps for Vespers.

Popularity: ♂ uncommon ↑

Legacy

Origin: in modern English, a legacy is that which is inherited by the family of one who has died. Ultimately it comes from Latin meaning "ambassador."

Significance: legacy also refers to the sum effect of the actions taken during one's life.

Popularity: uncommon ↑

Lucero

Origin: Spanish meaning "light," and also "morning star." Lucero is also the Spanish name for the planet Venus.

Significance: light is a symbol of goodness and truth.

Popularity: uncommon ↓

Makayla

Origin: alternate spelling of Michaela, the Germanic feminine of Michael, Hebrew meaning "Who is like God?"

Significance: Michael is an archangel whose defeat of Satan is described in the Book of Revelation.

Popularity: top 500 ↓

Spelling variations: *Mikayla, Michaela, Mikaela, Mckayla*

Cross-reference: The archangel Michael also plays a prominent role in the Book of Daniel. See chapter 1, "The Old Testament" (page 19).

Michelle

Origin: French feminine of Michael, Hebrew meaning "Who is like God?"

Significance: see Makayla.

Popularity: top 500 ↓

Related names:

Misha – nickname for Mikhail, a Russian form of Michael. In Russia it's traditionally a boys' name; in the US, however, it is more common for girls – endangered →

Cross-reference: Michelle and Misha are also listed in the section titled, "The Israelites in Exile" in chapter 1, "The Old Testament" (page 19).

Neveah (nev-AAY-uh)

Origin: *heaven* spelled backward.

Significance: see Heaven.

Popularity: top 500 ↑

Palmer

Origin: an English last name, given to a person who had a palm branch.

Significance: in medieval England, it was usual to bring back a palm branch as evidence of a pilgrimage to the Holy Land.

Popularity: ♂♀ uncommon ↑

Paloma

Origin: Spanish meaning "dove."

Significance: the dove is a symbol of peace and, especially in art, of the Holy Spirit.

Popularity: top 1000 →

Related names:

Dove – endangered →

Dovie – endangered →

Paradise

Origin: ultimately from a Persian word meaning "wall around," for an enclosed orchard or hunting preserve. It was borrowed into Greek and used in the Bible to refer to the Garden of Eden.

Significance: the Garden of Eden is the idyllic wilderness where Adam and Eve first lived. Paradise is also used in English to refer to heaven.

Popularity: endangered →

Pascale

Origin: from Latin *paschalis*, meaning "Easter." *Paschalis* is taken from Hebrew *Pesach*, meaning "Passover," because the two holidays fall close to one another in date.

Significance: Pascale is traditionally given to children born at Easter-time.

Popularity: spelled *Pascal* when used for boys – ♂♀ endangered ↓

Passion

Origin: Latin meaning "to suffer."

Significance: the Passion of Christ refers to the final days in the life of Jesus, from his triumphal entry into Jerusalem to the crucifixion.

Popularity: endangered →

Renata

Origin: feminine of the Latin name Renatus, meaning "re-born."

Significance: Renatus was used by early Christians as a reference to the resurrection of Jesus.

Popularity: top 1000 ↑

Renée

Origin: French meaning re-born.

Significance: see Renatus.

Popularity: spelled *René* when used for boys – ♂♀ top 1000 ↓

Related names:

Rena – endangered →

Seraphina

Origin: the Hebrew word *seraph* means "burning ones" and is generally a reference to serpents; however, in Isaiah 6: 1-3 the seraphs are winged beings of Heaven who stand by God.

Significance: Seraphina is a variation of *seraphim*, the Latin plural of *seraph*, the highest-ranking angels in heaven.

Popularity: uncommon ↑

Sunday

Origin: a Germanic translation of *dies Solis*, Latin meaning "sun's day."

Significance: the Christian sabbath.

Popularity: endangered ↑

Related names:

Dominique – French – uncommon ↓

Dominica – Italian – endangered →

Sybil

Origin: Greek meaning "prophetess." Sibyls were oracles in ancient Greece.

Significance: many sibylline prophecies have been interpreted as foretelling events such as the birth of Jesus and incidents in his life. Medieval Christian theology often treated sibyls as similar to Old Testament prophets.

Popularity: endangered ↑

Tiana

Origin: short form of Christiana, ultimately from Greek *khristos*, meaning "anointed."

Significance: see Christina.

Popularity: top 1000 →

Tina

Origin: short form of Christina.

Significance: see Christina.

Popularity: uncommon ↓

Tori

Origin: short form of Victoria, feminine of the Latin name Victor, meaning "conqueror."

Significance: see Victoria.

Popularity: top 1000 ↓

Trinity

Origin: Latin meaning "triple" and "triad."

Significance: the manifestation of God in the Father, Son, and Holy Ghost.

Popularity: top 500 ↓

Unity

Origin: Latin meaning "one."

Significance: a state in which all parts are joined together as one.

Popularity: endangered →

Veronica

Origin: Latin variation of the Greek name Pherenike meaning "bearer of victory."

Significance: according to tradition, when Jesus was carrying the cross Veronica gave him her veil, which he used to wipe his face. An image of his face then miraculously appeared on the veil. The name is also an anagram of *vera icon*, Latin meaning "true cross."

Popularity: top 500 ↓

Related names:

Ronnie – diminutive – endangered →

Veronique – French – endangered →

Berenice – an ancient Macedonian variation of Pherenike – endangered ↓

Cross-reference: Ronnie is also listed in chapter 5 (page 90).

Vesper

Origin: Latin meaning "evening star."

Significance: Vespers is the sunset prayer service for many Christians.

Popularity: endangered ↑

Victoria

Origin: feminine of the Latin name Victor, meaning "conqueror."

Significance: early Christians used the name Victor as a reference to Jesus's victory over death. Equally, it can imply strength of character, such as an ability to conquer temptation.

Popularity: top 100 →

Related names:

Vittoria – Italian – endangered →

Vicky – diminutive – endangered ↓

Victory – endangered ↑

Zoey

Origin: Greek meaning "life." Traditionally, it is spelled *Zoë*.

Significance: whereas *bios* is the physical life and *psuche* is the psychological life of intellect and emotion, *zoë* is the eternal life of God. The eternal life of man's soul is made possible by the sacrifice of Jesus.

Popularity: top 100 ↑

Spelling variations: *Zoë, Zoie*

Cross-reference: Zoë is also used as a name for Eve. See the section on "Genesis and Job" in chapter 1, "The Old Testament" (page 11).

Short Forms

Arlene

Origin: short form of several names ending with *-arlene*, such as Marlene, Charlene, and Darlene.

Popularity: uncommon ↓

Bella

Origin: short form of names ending with *-bella*.

Popularity: top 100 ↓

Related names:

Belle – French meaning "beautiful" – uncommon ↑

Cross-reference: Bella is also a short form of Isabella and is listed in chapter 2, "The New Testament" with the Elizabeth-names (page 42). The name is also listed in the section titled "Positive Characteristics" later in this chapter (page 60).

Ella

Origin: short form of names beginning with *el-*: Eleanor, Elizabeth, Ellen.

Popularity: top 100 ↓

Related names:

Ellarose – endangered ↑

Ellagrace – endangered →

Ellamae – endangered →

Ellamarie – endangered →

Ellarae – endangered →

Ellakate – endangered →

Elle

Origin: short forms of names beginning with *el-*: Eleanor, Elizabeth, Ellen.

Popularity: top 500 ↑

Ellie

Origin: diminutive of Elle and Ella.

Popularity: top 100 ↑

Related names:

Elliemae – endangered →

Etta

Origin: short forms of names ending with *-etta*: Loretta, Julietta, Henrietta, Concetta, Marietta.

Popularity: uncommon ↑

Gina

Origin: short form of names ending with *-gina*: Regina and Georgina

Popularity: uncommon ↓

Lena

Origin: short forms of names ending with *-lena*: Elena, Helena, Magdalena.

Popularity: top 1000 ↑

Lia

Origin: short forms of names ending with *-lia*: Julia, Natalia, Cecilia.

Popularity: top 500 ↑

Cross-reference: As a variant spelling of Leah, Lia is also listed in chapter 1, "The Old Testament" (page 10).

Lina

Origin: short forms of names ending with *-lina*: Angelina, Paulina.

Popularity: top 1000 ↑

Mena

Origin: short form of names ending with *-mena* or *-mina*: Philomena and Willamina.

Popularity: endangered →

Millie

Origin: diminutive of various names, including Mildred, Camilla, Emily.

Popularity: top 1000 ↑

Tia

Origin: short forms of names ending with –*tia*: Katia, Letitia.

Popularity: uncommon ↓

Traditional Virtues

Alba

Significance: Latin meaning "white," a color that implies purity.

Popularity: uncommon ↑

Bianca

Significance: Italian meaning "white," a color that implies purity.

Popularity: top 500 ↓

Related names:

Blanca – Spanish – uncommon ↓

Blanche – French – endangered →

Charity

Significance: showing loving kindness to others, often by material assistance to those in need.

Popularity: uncommon ↓

Chastity

Significance: being morally pure, especially in abstaining from sex.

Popularity: endangered →

Constance

Significance: resolute and unchanging faithfulness.

Popularity: uncommon ↓

Related names:

Constanza – Spanish – endangered →

Connie – diminutive – endangered ↓

Esperanza

Significance: Spanish meaning "hope."

Popularity: uncommon ↓

Faith

Significance: trust; belief without proof.

Popularity: top 100 ↓

Related names:

Faye – an Old English word meaning "faith" – top 1000 ↑

Frankie

Significance: diminutive of Frank, meaning direct and honest. Frank originally referred to a Frank, one of the powerful Germanic people who conquered the Celts in what is now France. As members of the ruling class, the Franks were able to speak freely, giving rise to the current meaning "direct and honest."

Popularity: ♂ uncommon ↑

Cross-reference: Frankie is also used as a short form of Frances. See the section titled "Saints of the Middle Ages" in chapter 5 (page 86).

Gwen

Significance: Welsh meaning "white," a color that implies purity.

Popularity: top 1000 ↑

Honesty

Significance: being free of deceit; not telling lies.

Popularity: uncommon ↑

Honor

Significance: in an internal sense, being honorable is having great moral integrity. The usual Biblical sense is more external—it is giving respect and obedience, as to God, parents, and laws.

Popularity: uncommon ↑

Hope

Significance: an expectation that a desired event will come to pass.

Popularity: top 500 ↓

Ivory

Significance: a creamy white color that implies purity.

Popularity: top 1000 ↑

Justice

Significance: the fair treatment of people, especially under the law.

Popularity: ♂ top 500 ↑

Justine

Significance: feminine of Justin, a short form of Justinian. Justinian is a Latin name meaning justice.

Popularity: uncommon ↓

Related names:

Justina – endangered ↓

Love

Significance: great affection and care.

Popularity: uncommon ↑

Related names:

Lovella – endangered →

Lovie – endangered →

Loyalty

Significance: unyielding faithfulness.

Popularity: endangered ↑

Related names:

Loyal – endangered ↑

Mercy

Significance: compassion to people in need or to those who have behaved wrongly.

Popularity: top 1000 ↑

Related names:

Merry – used by Charles Dickens as a nickname for Mercy – endangered →

Modesty

Significance: proper and reserved behavior.

Popularity: endangered →

Nadia

Significance: Slavic meaning "hope."

Popularity: top 500 ↓

Related names:

Nadine – French variation of Nadia – uncommon →

Noble

Significance: having an exceptionally good character and high ideals.

Popularity: ♂ endangered →

Nora

Significance: short form of Honora, meaning "honored," respected for great or noble deeds.

Popularity: top 100 ↑

Related names:

Honora – variation of the Latin name Honoria – endangered →

Spelling variations: *Norah*

Patience

Significance: calm acceptance of trouble or delay.

Popularity: top 1000 ↓

Pia

Significance: Latin meaning "pious."

Popularity: endangered ↑

Prudence

Significance: wise and careful action.

Popularity: endangered ↑

Sage

Significance: wise.

Popularity: top 500 →

Sincere

Significance: honestly expressing one's thoughts and feelings.

Popularity: ♂ endangered →

Temperance

Significance: moderating one's feelings, thoughts, and actions.

Popularity: top 1000 ↑

Truly

Significance: honestly, faithfully.

Popularity: endangered ↑

Related names:

Tru – ♂♀ endangered ↓

Truth – ♂♀ endangered →

Vera

Significance: Latin meaning "true." In many Slavic languages it has the connotation of "faith."

Popularity: top 500 ↑

Verity

Significance: honesty, truthfulness.

Popularity: endangered ↑

Wisdom

Significance: acting with insight and good judgment.

Popularity: endangered →

Zuri

Significance: Basque meaning "white," a color that implies purity.

Popularity: top 500 ↑

Positive Characteristics

The names we give our children often reflect the qualities we want to see in them. Many girls' names repeat themes of serenity, happiness, sweetness, and beauty.

Alaia

Origin: Basque.
Meaning: happy.
Popularity: endangered ↑

Allegra

Origin: Italian.
Meaning: happy, lively.
Popularity: endangered →

Beautiful

Origin: Latin.
Meaning: charming and delightful.
Popularity: endangered →

Bella

Origin: Italian.
Meaning: beautiful.
Popularity: top 100 ↓
Related names:

Belle – French – uncommon ↑

Miabella – "my beautiful girl" – endangered ↑

Belladonna – "pretty lady" – endangered →

Labella – "the beautiful girl – endangered →

Cross-reference: Bella is also listed in chapter 2 (page 42) and in a previous section of this chapter (page 56).

Blessed

Origin: Old English.
Meaning: given gifts from God.
Popularity: endangered →

Bliss

Origin: Old English.
Meaning: enduring happiness.
Popularity: endangered →

Blythe

Origin: Old English.
Meaning: happy and carefree.
Popularity: uncommon ↑

Bonita

Origin: Spanish.
Meaning: pretty.
Popularity: endangered →

Bonnie

Origin: Scottish.
Meaning: pretty.
Popularity: top 1000 ↑

Candy

Origin: Sanskrit.
Meaning: a sweet confection.
Popularity: endangered ↓

Charisma

Origin: a German construct based on Charis, the Greek name for any one of the three Charities (Graces), and also an alternate name for Aglaia, the Greek goddess of beauty and adornment.
Meaning: a personal quality that attracts others, inspiring exceptional enthusiasm, affection, or loyalty.
Popularity: endangered ↓

Dream

Origin: Germanic.

Meaning: originally for the images that pass through the mind during sleep, but now also meaning that which one has long wished for.

Popularity: endangered →

Dulce (DUL-seh)

Origin: Spanish.

Meaning: sweet.

Popularity: top 1000 ↓

Essence

Origin: Latin.

Meaning: the spiritual nature of a thing that makes it what it is.

Popularity: uncommon ↓

Farah

Origin: Arabic.

Meaning: joy.

Popularity: uncommon →

Felicia (fuh-LEESH-uh)

Origin: Latin.

Meaning: happy, fortunate.

Popularity: endangered ↓

Felicity

Origin: Latin.

Meaning: happy, especially in one's domestic life.

Popularity: top 500 →

Gala

Origin: French.

Meaning: an especially grand, elaborate, and elegant celebration.

Popularity: endangered ↑

Harmony

Origin: Greek.

Meaning: a pleasant and peaceful relationship; a pleasing combination, particularly of sound.

Popularity: top 500 ↑

Honey

Origin: Old English.

Meaning: a term of endearment; the sweet substance produced by bees.

Popularity: endangered ↓

Jolie

Origin: French.

Meaning: pretty.

Popularity: top 1000 ↓

Joy

Origin: French.

Meaning: great happiness.

Popularity: top 500 ↑

Jubilee

Origin: French.

Meaning: a celebration, especially an anniversary, and particularly the 25th or 50th anniversary.

Popularity: uncommon ↑

Lana

Origin: Hawaiian.

Meaning: calm, with reference to water, such as still water or that which floats in water.

Popularity: top 500 ↑

Liberty

Origin: Latin.

Meaning: the power to act without constraint.

Popularity: top 1000 →

Linda

Origin: short form of Germanic names containing the element *linde*, "tender," such as Erminlinda, "wholly tender" or Roslind, "horse tender."

Meaning: coincidentally, *linda* means "pretty" in Spanish, and is often given in the US with that intended meaning.

Popularity: top 1000 ↓

Lovely

Origin: Old English.

Meaning: charmingly pretty.

Popularity: endangered →

Lucky

Origin: Germanic.

Meaning: enjoying good fortune.

Popularity: endangered →

Lulu

Origin: Hawaiian.

Meaning: calm, with a connotation of protection, such as a ship in a harbor or a restful sea.

Popularity: endangered →

Malina (muh-LEE-nuh)

Origin: Hawaiian.

Meaning: calming, soothing.

Popularity: uncommon →

Related names:

    Mālie (MAH-lee-eh) – Hawaiian meaning "quiet, still" – endangered →

Maple

Origin: Old English.

Meaning: syrup from the sweet sap of the maple tree.

Popularity: endangered ↑

Merry

Origin: Old English.

Meaning: festive and joyful; in the US the word is strongly associated with Christmas.

Popularity: endangered →

Mirabelle

Origin: from the Latin root *mirari*, meaning "admire" and "wonder at."

Meaning: wonderful.

Popularity: endangered ↑

Related names:

    Mirabella – endangered →

Miya

Origin: Japanese.

Meaning: beautiful.

Popularity: top 1000 →

Providence

Origin: Latin.

Meaning: the guidance and care provided by God.

Popularity: endangered ↑

Raya

Origin: Latin.

Meaning: often taken as "a ray of sunshine," though it originated as a Slavic diminutive for names such as Raisa, Regina, and Radko.

Popularity: uncommon ↑

Rejoice

Origin: Latin.

Meaning: celebrate something that has brought great happiness.

Popularity: endangered →

Serena

Origin: Latin.

Meaning: clear and tranquil.

Popularity: top 500 ↓

Serenity

Origin: Latin.

Meaning: calm and peaceful.

Popularity: top 100 ↑

Related names:

Serene – endangered →

Sol

Origin: Latin.

Meaning: the name of the star at the center of our solar system.

Popularity: endangered →

Soleil

Origin: French.

Meaning: sun.

Popularity: uncommon →

Sparkle

Origin: Middle English.

Meaning: reflect flashes of light.

Popularity: endangered →

Sunny

Origin: Old English.

Meaning: bright and cloudless.

Popularity: uncommon ↑

Related names:

Sunshine – endangered ↓

Unique

Origin: Latin.

Meaning: that which has no duplicate, nothing that is like or equal to it.

Popularity: uncommon ↓

Love Names

There is a strong Christian tradition for using love names. In fact, Love was the name of an early martyr (translated from the Greek name Agape). And Truelove Brewster was a passenger on the *Mayflower*. Some love-names, particularly Blessing and Promise, recall God's love for man; others, such as Cherish, Darlene, and Precious, evoke the more earthly love of a parent for a child.

Amity

Origin: Latin.

Meaning: a friendly relationship.

Popularity: endangered →

Amora

Origin: Spanish, feminine of Amor.

Meaning: love.

Popularity: uncommon ↑

Related names:

Amor – uncommon ↑

Amorette – endangered →

Amy

Origin: English form of French *aimée*.

Meaning: beloved.

Popularity: top 500 →

Annabelle

Origin: variation of Amabel, a medieval French form of the Latin name Amabilis.

Meaning: loveable.

Popularity: top 100 ↑

Related names:

Annabella – top 500 ↑

Annebelle – endangered ↑

Spelling variations: *Annabel, Annabell*

Cross-reference: Amabilis is also saints' names. See the section titled "Saints of the Middle Ages" in chapter 5 (page 82).

Arabella

Origin: Scottish variation of Annabelle.

Meaning: loveable.

Popularity: top 500 ↑

Related names:

Arabelle – uncommon ↑

Blessing

Origin: Old English.

Meaning: a gift from God that makes one very happy.

Popularity: uncommon ↑

Cherish

Origin: French.

Meaning: to love dearly.

Popularity: top 500 ↓

Corazón

Origin: Spanish.

Meaning: heart

Popularity: endangered →

Darlene

Origin: Old English.

Meaning: dear one.

Popularity: uncommon ↓

Related names:

Darla – uncommon ↑

Favor

Origin: Latin.

Meaning: show approval or preference; a kind or generous deed.

Popularity: endangered →

Jadore

Origin: French.

Meaning: I love or I adore.

Popularity: endangered ↑

Love

Origin: Old English.

Meaning: great affection and care.

Popularity: uncommon ↑

Mabel

Origin: short form of the medieval French name Amabel, from the Latin name Amabilis.

Meaning: loveable.

Popularity: endangered ↑

Cross-reference: Amabilis and Mabel are also saints' names. See the section titled "Saints of the Middle Ages" in chapter 5 (page 89).

Mandy

Origin: diminutive of Amanda, Latin, feminine of Amandus.

Meaning: worthy of love.

Popularity: uncommon ↓

Related names:

Amanda – endangered ↓

Cross-reference: Because Amandus is also a saints' name, Mandy is listed in the section titled "Saints of the Middle Ages" in chapter 5 (page 89).

Miracle

Origin: Latin.

Meaning: a wonderful event that defies nature and is attributed to divine intervention.

Popularity: top 500 ↑

Related names:

Amiracle – endangered →

Precious

Origin: Latin.

Meaning: a thing that is both rare and extremely important.

Popularity: uncommon ↓

Promise

Origin: Latin.

Meaning: a pledge to commit, or to refrain from committing, a specific action. The name calls to mind both human honesty and loyalty, and the covenants between God and man.

Popularity: uncommon ↑

Sherry

Origin: English spelling of the French word *cherie*.

Meaning: dear.

Popularity: endangered ↓

Treasure

Origin: Latin.

Meaning: a store of riches.

Popularity: uncommon ↑

Chapter 4: Early Martyrs

Adrienne

Origin: feminine spelling of Adrian, a variation of Hadrian, the name of the great Roman emperor from the town of Hadria, in Italy.

Significance: Adrian was a member of the imperial guard of the Roman emperor Maximian. He converted while participating in the torture of Christians and was himself imprisoned and later martyred.

Popularity: top 1000 →

Related names:

Adriana – top 500 ↓

Adria – endangered →

Agatha

Origin: Greek meaning "good."

Significance: a fifteen-year-old girl who dedicated her virginity to God. She was martyred c. 251 during a wave of Christian persecutions.

Popularity: endangered ↑

Agata – endangered →

Agnes

Origin: Greek meaning "pure."

Significance: born into a wealthy Christian family. Tradition has it that she was denounced by a rejected suitor and was martyred when she was about 12 years old.

Popularity: uncommon ↑

Related names:

Anniston – originally an English last name meaning "Agnes's settlement": Annis was the medieval

English pronunciation of Agnes – top 1000 ↑

Ines – form of Agnes used in several Romance languages – endangered →

Inez – English variation of Ines – endangered →

Alexandra

Origin: Greek meaning "defender of men."

Significance: the wife of the emperor Diocletian. During the torture of the martyr George, Alexandra went into the arena and bowed down to him, thus declaring the faith she had kept secret. She was then immediately killed on the orders of her husband.

Popularity: top 100 ↓

Related names:

Alexa – short form – top 100 →

Alessandra – Italian – top 500 ↑

Alejandra – Spanish – top 500 ↓

Alex – short form – ♂ uncommon →

Allie

Origin: short form of Alexandra.

Significance: see Alexandra.

Popularity: top 500 ↓

Spelling variations: *Ally*

Cross-reference: Allie is also listed in chapter 5, in the section titled "Saints of the Middle Ages" (page 81).

Anastasia

Origin: Greek meaning "resurrection."

Significance: a woman from the Roman province of Pannonia (now in Serbia) who was martyred on Christmas day.

Popularity: top 500 →

Related names:

Anya – top 500 →

Stacy – uncommon ↓

Cross-reference: Anastasia is also listed in chapter 3 (page 49).

Apollonia

Origin: from Apollo, the name of a Greek god.

Significance: a deaconess of the Church in Alexandria. She was martyred by a mob in a general uprising of the people against Christians.

Popularity: endangered →

Related names:

Pola – Polish short form – endangered ↑

Ariadne

Origin: Greek meaning "most holy."

Significance: a slave in the house of a prince of Phrygia (now in Turkey). She fell into a chasm and died as she fled from persecution for having refused to participate in pagan rites celebrating the prince's birthday.

Popularity: top 1000 ↑

Related names:

Ariadna – uncommon →

Ariana

Origin: variation of Ariadne, Greek meaning "most holy."

Significance: see Ariadne.

Popularity: top 100 →

Related names:

Ariane – uncommon ↑

Arianny – uncommon →

Arionna – uncommon →

Spelling variations: *Arianna*

Barbara

Origin: Greek meaning "foreign."

Significance: born to pagans in the third century. She was martyred by her father in 304 when she revealed her faith. Barbara was killed alongside the martyr Juliana, whose circumstances were very similar.

Popularity: top 1000 ↓

Beatrice (BEE-uh-triss)

Origin: the Latin name Viatrix, which means "voyager/traveler," came to be associated with the unrelated Latin word *beatus*, meaning "blessed." This caused the initial *v* to become a *b*, resulting in the form Beatrix, of which Beatrice is a variation.

Significance: Beatrice is an Italian and French variation of Beatrix who, after her brothers were martyred, helped many persecuted Christians before being denounced in 303 by a neighbor who wanted her land.

Popularity: top 1000 ↑

Related names:

Beatrix (BEE-uh-tricks) – an older form of Beatrice – uncommon ↑

Beatriz (bey-ah-TREEZ) – Iberian form of Beatrix – uncommon ↓

Trixie – nickname for Beatrix – endangered →

Catalina

Origin: variation of Katherine, used in several Romance languages.

Significance: see Katherine.

Popularity: top 500 ↑

Spelling variations: *Katalina*

Cecilia

Origin: both the name of an ancient Roman family and its feminine form.

Significance: a woman from a patrician family who was told by an angel not to consummate her marriage to a pagan man. Her husband converted to Christianity, after which he also saw the angel. Both were martyred by a Roman prefect between 176 and 180.

Popularity: top 500 ↑

Related names:

Cecily – short form – uncommon ↑

Sheila – Irish – uncommon ↓

Spelling variations: *Cecelia*

Charity

Origin: from Latin *caritas*, which is a translation of Greek *agape*, meaning "brotherly love and kindness."

Significance: one of three young sisters who were martyred together. Three days later, their mother, Sophia, who is also considered a martyr, died upon the graves of her daughters: Faith, Hope, and Charity (sometimes translated as Love).

Popularity: uncommon ↓

Daria

Origin: feminine of Darius, the great king of the Achaemenid Empire. The name is Persian meaning "he holds (possesses)," from a longer name meaning "holds firm the good."

Significance: a Roman vestal virgin who married a Christian from a pagan family and then converted. They were martyred c. 283 for converting others to their faith.

Popularity: uncommon ↓

Denise

Origin: feminine of Dennis.

Significance: Dennis was martyred around the year 250. He was the bishop of Paris at the time and is considered a patron saint of that city.

Popularity: top 1000 ↓

Donatella

Origin: feminine diminutive of Donato, which is the Italian form of Donatus, Latin meaning "given."

Significance: Donato was a 4th century bishop who was martyred under Julian the Apostate. Julian was a Roman emperor who outlawed Christianity after Constantine I had declared it legal.

Popularity: endangered →

Dorothy

Origin: short form of Dorothea, Greek meaning "gift of God": *doron*, "gift" + *theos*, "god." Theodora comprises the same elements in reverse order.

Significance: there were two martyrs named Dorothea: 1) a young virgin from a Christian family who was martyred in 311; 2) a girl from a noble family who is said to have rejected as a suitor the emperor Maximus in order to remain Christian. She was martyred in 320.

Popularity: top 1000 ↑

Related names:

Thea – short form of Dorothea and Theodora – top 1000 ↑

Tea (TAY-uh) – variation of Thea – endangered ↓

Teddi – diminutive of Ted, a short from of the masculine equivalent, Theodore – endangered →

Dolly – nickname for Dorothy – endangered →

Theodora – endangered ↑

Dorothea – endangered →

Dora – short form of Dorothea and Theodora – endangered ↓

Effie

Origin: diminutive of Euphemia, Greek meaning "she who others speak well of."

Significance: Euphemia was a Greek virgin who was killed in the arena after refusing to sacrifice to pagan gods. She was martyred in 303 under a general persecution ordered by the emperor Diocletian.

Popularity: endangered ↑

Related names:

Euphemia – endangered →

Elaine

Origin: French form of Eleanor, which is a variation of Helen.

Significance: see Helen.

Popularity: top 1000 →

Related names:

Elena – variation – top 500 ↑

Lainey – nickname – top 1000 →

Laina – short form – uncommon ↑

Eleanor

Origin: variation of Helen.

Significance: see Helen.

Popularity: top 100 ↑

Related names:

Lenora – short form – endangered ↑

Nelly – diminutive – uncommon →

Elenora – elaboration – endangered →

Hannelore – German combination of Hanna + Eleonore – endangered →

Ellen

Origin: variation of Helen.

Significance: see Helen.

Popularity: top 1000 ↓

Related names:

Elina – Scandinavian – uncommon ↑

Ila – contraction of Elina – uncommon ↑

Eulalia

Origin: Greek meaning "well-spoken."

Significance: a young girl martyred under a general persecution ordered by the emperor Diocletian.

Popularity: endangered →

Fabiola

Origin: feminine of Fabian, from Fabia, a patrician Roman family name.

Significance: as pope, Fabian was a conciliatory figure who generally maintained good relations with the Roman government; however, he was martyred during a widespread persecution of Christians in 250.

Popularity: uncommon ↓

Related names:

Fabiana – endangered →

Faith

Origin: Faith is Latin meaning "trust; belief without proof."

Significance: Faith (Greek Pistis, Latin Fides) was one of three young sisters who were martyred together. Three days later, their mother, Sophia, who is also considered a martyr, died upon the graves of her daughters: Faith, Hope, and Love (also called Charity).

Popularity: top 100 ↓

Related names:

Faye – an Old English word meaning "faith" – uncommon ↑

Georgia

Origin: feminine of George, Greek meaning "farmer."

Significance: George was born into Christian family and served as a soldier in the Roman army. He was martyred as part of an edict to purge the army of Christians. As he was tortured in the arena, more than 600 people either revealed their faith or converted on the spot. All were subsequently martyred themselves, including the empress Alexandra, who revealed her faith by entering the arena and bowing down to George, upon which both were immediately killed on the orders of the emperor, Diocletian.

Popularity: top 500 ↑

Georgina – feminine – uncommon →

Gina – Italian diminutive of Georgina – uncommon ↓

Georgie – English diminutive – endangered →

Georgette – French feminine – endangered →

Georgiana – English feminine – endangered ↑

Gigi – French diminutive of Georgine – endangered →

Cross-reference: Georgia is also listed in chapter 5, "Saints" (page 86).

Greta

Origin: German contracted short form of Margareta.

Significance: see Margaret.

Popularity: top 1000 ↑

Related names:

Gretchen – uncommon ↓

Gretel – endangered ↑

Helen

Origin: Greek meaning "light."

Significance: a young Spanish woman who came to the defense of another Christian, Centrolla, as she was being harassed in the street. The women were martyred together in 304.

Popularity: top 500 →

Related names:

Helena – variation – top 1000 →

Eleni – modern Greek form – uncommon →

Cross-reference: Helena is also the name of an early saint. See the section titled "The Church to 500 AD" in chapter 5 (page 79).

Hermione

Origin: Greek meaning "daughter of Hermes."

Significance: a prophetess and healer who was martyred in 117 during a widespread persecution of Christians.

Popularity: endangered →

Hope

Origin: Germanic meaning, "an expectation that a desired event will come to pass."

Significance: Hope (Greek Elpis, Latin Spes) was one of three young sisters who were martyred together. Three days later, their mother, Sophia, who is also considered a martyr, died upon the graves of her daughters: Faith, Hope, and Love (also called Charity).

Popularity: top 500 ↓

Irene

Origin: Greek meaning "peace."

Significance: there were four martyrs named Irene, the earliest of whom was born in the first century and was baptized by Timothy.

Popularity: top 1000 →

Related names:

Irina – endangered ↑

Jovita

Origin: Latin meaning "dedicated to Jove."

Significance: Jovita was martyred with his brother, Faustinus, in 120 for preaching the Gospel.

Popularity: endangered ↓

Related names:

Jovie – uncommon ↑

Julia

Origin: both the name of an ancient Roman family and its feminine form.

Significance: a devout virgin from the island that is now Corsica. Being a Christian, Julia was sold as a slave, but she was such a valuable servant that her master would not torture or martyr her. However, a tribune ordered her to sacrifice to pagan gods and, when she would not, had her killed.

Popularity: top 100 ↓

Related names:

Julie – short form – top 500 ↓

Julissa – Spanish variation – top 500 ↓

Jules – French form of Julius, the masculine of Julia. Traditionally it's a boys' name, but in the US it's used in equal numbers for girls and boys. – ♂♀ endangered →

Juliana

Origin: feminine of Julian, from the ancient Roman family name.

Significance: a Greek woman born to pagan parents. She would not renounce her faith in order to marry, so her father denounced her and she was martyred in 304 alongside the martyr Barbara, whose circumstances were very similar.

Popularity: top 500 →

Related names:

Julianne – another feminine of Julian – top 1000 ↓

Julian – from Julia – ♂ endangered ↓

Julianny – diminutive – endangered →

Julionna – variation – endangered →

Spelling variations: *Julianna*

Juliet

Origin: Juliet and Julieta are diminutives of Julia, which is both the name of an ancient Roman family and its feminine form.

Significance: Julieta was a Greek woman who was martyred with her young son, Quiricus, in 304.

Popularity: top 500 ↑

Related names:

Julieta – top 1000 ↑

Julieth – endangered ↑

Justine

Origin: short form of Justina, feminine of Justinus, Latin meaning "just."

Significance: a young woman from a good family who had dedicated her virginity to God and converted at least two of her admirers to her faith. She was martyred in 305.

Popularity: uncommon ↓

Related names:

Justina – endangered ↓

Kaitlyn

Origin: Irish form of Katherine. In Ireland it is usually spelled *Caitlin* (there is no *k* in the Irish alphabet). Occasionally it is now also spelled *Katelyn*, but no other spellings are used in Ireland.

Significance: see Katherine.

Popularity: top 500 ↓

Spelling variations: *Katelyn, Caitlyn, Caitlin, Katelynn, Kaitlynn*

Karen

Origin: Scandinavian contraction of Katherine.

Significance: see Katherine.

Popularity: top 500 ↓

Related names:

Kalena – Hawaiian form of Karen based on similar pronunciation; it means "yellowish one" in Hawaiian – endangered →

Katherine

Origin: form the Greek name Aikaterine, the meaning of which is unknown. The *th* was added to English spellings by Renaissance grammarians in a mistaken belief that the name was related to the Greek word *kathos*, meaning "pure."

Significance: a pagan-born woman who dedicated her virginity to Jesus and converted many people to her faith. She and all of the people she converted were martyred in 305.

Popularity: top 100 ↓

Related names:

Kate – top 500 →

Katie – top 500 ↓

Kathy – uncommon ↓

Kay – endangered →

Kit – endangered →

Spelling variations: *Catherine, Kathryn*

Kathleen

Origin: English spelling of Kaitlyn, representing the Irish pronunciation.

Significance: see Katherine.

Popularity: top 1000 ↓

Katrina

Origin: Germanic and Slavic form of Katherine.

Significance: see Katherine.

Popularity: uncommon ↓

Related names:

Katia – uncommon ↓

Katerina – uncommon →

Trina – endangered ↓

Larissa

Origin: Greek meaning "fortress."

Significance: she and about 300 other Christians were martyred by the Goths in the 4ᵗʰ century.

Popularity: uncommon ↓

Lexi

Origin: short form of Alexandra, Greek meaning "protector, defender."

Significance: see Alexandra.

Popularity: top 500 ↑

Related names:

Lexa – English – endangered →

Lexia – English – endangered ↓

Lexis – English – endangered ↓

Spelling variations: *Lexie*

Cross-reference: Because Lexi is a short form of Alexis, she is also listed in chapter 5, "Saints" (page 88).

Love

Origin: Germanic meaning "great affection."

Significance: Love (Greek Agape, Latin Caritas) was one of three young sisters who were martyred together. Three days later, their mother, Sophia, who is also considered a martyr, died upon the graves of her daughters:

Faith, Hope, and Love (sometimes called Charity).

Popularity: uncommon ↑

Lucy

Origin: English short form of Lucia, a feminine of Lucius, Latin meaning "light." Lucie was used by the Etruscans (an ancient Italian people) as a masculine name more than 1000 years before the English form came into use.

Significance: Lucia was from a patrician family and dedicated her virginity to God. She gave much of her inheritance to help the poor before being denounced by her betrothed husband in 304.

Popularity: top 100 ↑

Related names:

Lucia – top 500 ↑

Lucille – top 500 ↑

Luciana – top 500 ↑

Lucinda – uncommon →

Lucienne – endangered ↑

Lucina – endangered →

Lucila – endangered ↓

Maggie

Origin: English diminutive of Margaret.

Significance: see Margaret.

Popularity: top 500 ↓

Related names:

Meggie – endangered →

Peggy – nickname for Meggie. In England, rhyming was once a popular source of nicknames – endangered →

Margaret

Origin: English short form of Margarita.

Significance: Margaret the Virgin was a woman from a pagan family. She was martyred in 304 by a wealthy Roman who wanted her to renounce her faith and marry him.

Popularity: top 500 →

Related names:

Maisie – Scottish – top 1000 ↑

May – English and Scottish – uncommon ↑

Marjorie – English spelling that reflects the usual pronunciation of Margaret in medieval England – endangered ↑

Cross-reference: May is also a listed as one of Mary's related names in chapter 2, "The New Testament" (page 30).

Margarita

Origin: Latin form of the Greek word *margarites*, meaning "pearl."

Significance: see Margaret.

Popularity: uncommon ↓

Related names:

Rita – short form – uncommon →

Magaly – Catalan – endangered ↓

Cross-reference: Rita is also the name of a 15th century Italian saint. See chapter 5 "Saints" (page 89).

Margot

Origin: French nickname for Marguerite.

Significance: see Margaret.

Popularity: top 1000 ↑

Related names:

Marguerite – endangered →

Marina

Origin: Orthodox name of Margaret the Virgin.

Significance: see Margaret.

Popularity: top 1000 ↓

Related names:

Marin – short form – uncommon ↓

Marnie – diminutive of Marna, a Scandinavian form of Marina – endangered →

Martina

Origin: feminine of Martin, from the Roman family name Martinus.

Significance: an orphan martyred in 228 during widespread persecutions.

Popularity: uncommon →

Megan

Origin: Welsh diminutive of Meg.

Significance: see Margaret.

Popularity: top 500 ↓

Related names:

Meg – Scottish short form of Margaret – endangered ↓

Philomena

Origin: Greek meaning "lover of strength."

Significance: martyred when she was about 13 years old in a widespread persecution of Christians. Memory of her martyrdom was lost until her tomb was re-discovered in 1802.

Popularity: endangered ↑

Related names:

Mena – short form of Willamina and Philomena – endangered →

Regina

Origin: Latin meaning "queen."

Significance: born to pagan parents in what is now France. She would not renounce her faith in order to marry and so was martyred.

Popularity: endangered →

Related names:

Gina – Italian diminutive of names ending with –*gina* – uncommon ↓

Sabina

Origin: the Sabines were an ancient people of Italy.

Significance: Sabina was the widow of a Roman senator. She was converted by one of her slaves, who was later martyred. Sabina buried the slave's remains in the family mausoleum, for which she too was denounced and martyred.

Popularity: uncommon →

Related names:

Sabine – endangered →

Sandra

Origin: nickname for Alexandra.

Significance: see Alexandra.

Popularity: top 1000 ↓

Related names:

Sandy – diminutive – uncommon ↓

Sasha

Origin: Slavic diminutive of Aleksandra.

Significance: see Alexandra.

Popularity: in Russian tradition it is more common for boys than girls, but in the US it is used almost exclusively for girls – top 1000 ↓

Sheila

Origin: Irish form of Cecilia, which is both the name of an ancient Roman family and its feminine form.

Significance: see Cecilia.

Popularity: uncommon ↓

Related names:

Shyla – uncommon ↓

Shayla – endangered ↓

Sonia

Origin: Slavic and Scandinavian nickname for Sophia, Greek meaning "wisdom."

Significance: see Sophia.

Popularity: top 500 ↓

Sophia

Origin: Greek meaning "wisdom."

Significance: there were three martyrs named Sophia. The earliest was a possibly legendary woman who died on the graves of her three young daughters, Faith, Hope, and Love (also called Charity), after their martyrdom.

Popularity: top 10 ↓

Related names:

Zofia – Slavic – endangered →

Sophina – endangered →

Anasofia – endangered ↑

Sophiagrace – endangered ↑

Sophiarose – endangered →

Sophiamarie – endangered →

Spelling variations: *Sofia*

Sophie

Origin: diminutive of Sophia.

Significance: see Sophia.

Popularity: top 100 ↓

Stephanie

Origin: feminine of Stephen, Greek meaning "wreath," implying an honor bestowed.

Significance: Stephen was a teacher and active member of the early Church. He was a Jewish convert and is believed to be the first Christian martyr, put to death by Jewish authorities for blasphemy.

Popularity: top 500 ↓

Related names:

Stevie – top 1000 ↑

Estefania – uncommon ↓

Estefany – uncommon ↓

Stephania – endangered ↓

Sydney

Origin: contraction of Saint Denis.

Significance: see Denise.

Popularity: Sidney is traditionally a boys' name, but now it's more common for girls. The spelling *Sidney* is slightly more popular for girls than boys while *Sydney* is used almost exclusively for girls. ♂♀ top 500 ↓

Spelling variations: *Sidney*

Tatiana

Origin: feminine of Tatianus, a Roman family name from the legendary Sabine king Titus Tatianus.

Significance: born to a Christian family, Tatiana became a deaconess in the Roman church. She was martyred in the early 3rd century.

Popularity: top 1000 ↓

Related names:

Tania – uncommon ↓

Valentina

Origin: feminine of Valentinus, from Latin meaning "strong."

Significance: there are three saints named Valentine, all martyred at different times and in different places. Their feast day is celebrated on February 14. The first recorded connection between Saint Valentine's Day and romance occurs in Geoffrey Chaucer's 1382 poem titled "Parlement of Foules." There may have been a remnant of an older pagan fertility or marriage festival near the saints' feast day.

Popularity: top 500 ↑

Related names:

Valentine – ♂♀ endangered ↑

Vita

Origin: feminine of Vitus, Latin meaning "life."

Significance: Vitus was martyred when he was 12-13 years old under the emperor Diocletian in 303.

Popularity: endangered ↑

Vitalia

Origin: feminine of Vitalis, Latin meaning "of life."

Significance: there were three martyrs named Vitalis: 1) Vitalis of Milan, who was killed in the 1st or 2nd century; 2) a man named Vitalis who was martyred under a general persecution in 250; 3) a slave who was converted by his master, Agricola, with whom he developed a close friendship. He was killed in an amphitheater under the emperor Diocletian in 304.

Popularity: endangered →

Vivian (VIV-ee-uhn)

Origin: short form of Viviana, feminine of Vivianus, a Roman family name meaning "living, alive."

Significance: Viviana was a young virgin martyred with her family in 460 under a persecution ordered by the emperor Julian.

Popularity: top 100 ↑

Related names:

Viviana – older form of Vivian – top 500 →

Vivianne (viv-ee-ANN) – variation of Vivian – uncommon ↑

Bibiana – variation of Viviana – endangered ↓

Xenia

Origin: Greek meaning "hospitality."

Significance: born into a Christian family, Xenia was martyred in 4th century Greece by a pagan government official whose proposal of marriage she had rejected.

Popularity: endangered →

Related names:

Oksana – Ukrainian form of Xenia – endangered ↓

Zenaida

Origin: from Zenais, a Greek name meaning "of Zeus."

Significance: a very early convert who, with her sister Philonella, became a physician. The sisters charged patients only what they could afford to pay. They died c. 100. Some accounts indicate that they were martyred; others say that they died of natural causes.

Popularity: endangered →

Chapter 5: Saints

As you look through the names in this chapter, keep in mind that I wrote this book to help Christian couples find baby names. I didn't think it would be helpful to list every saint's name that's ever been. After all, no American parent has ever named a little boy Austriclinian or a little girl Cunegundes—two of the many never-used names I've seen in other Christian baby name books. Rather, my goal is to provide a comprehensive list of the Christian names currently used in the US. I've tried to give a general sense of the history of each name, with its meaning and popularity.

Santina

Origin: feminine diminutive of *santo*, "saint" in several Romance languages.

Significance: "saint" is an official title given by the Church in memory of those whose actions have demonstrated extraordinary holiness.

Popularity: endangered →

Related names:

Santa – endangered →

The Church to 500 AD

Aurelia

Origin: feminine of Aurelius, Latin meaning "golden."

Significance: Aurelius was an influential Roman bishop who led several early councils on doctrine.

Popularity: top 1000 ↑

Austyn

Origin: contraction of Augustine, a diminutive of Augustus, which means "majestic." Augustus was a title of the first Roman emperor and, therefore, of many later emperors.

Significance: Saint Augustine was a 4th century theologian and philosopher of northern Africa. His extremely influential *City of God* and *Confessions of St. Augustine* are still widely read.

Popularity: All together, Austen and its many spelling variations are much more popular for boys than for girls. When used for girls, however, *Austyn* is the most common spelling. – ♂ uncommon ↑

Bryce

Origin: blend of *ap Rhys*, Welsh meaning "son of Rhys." Rhys means "enthusiasm" in Welsh.

Significance: in the 5th century, Saint Brice was an orphan raised by Saint Martin. He was exiled for seven years for immoral behavior, but after a long period of repentance, he became a humble and pious man and was made bishop of Tours, a city in France.

Popularity: ♂ endangered →

Clementine

Origin: a feminine of Clement, Latin meaning "gentle."

Significance: Clement was a companion of Peter and Paul. He was ordained bishop by Peter and became the fourth pope, from 92-99. At least thirteen later popes were also named Clement.

Popularity: top 1000 ↑

Related names:

Clementina – endangered →

Clemence – French – endangered →

Colette

Origin: short form of Nicolette, a French diminutive of Nicole.

Significance: see Nicole.

Popularity: top 1000 ↑

Related names:

Nicolette – uncommon ↓

Collins

Origin: Scottish short form of Nicholas, Greek meaning "victory of the people."

Significance: see Nicole.

Popularity: top 1000 ↑

Emilia

Origin: spelling variation of Aemilia, which is both a Roman family name and its feminine form. Surprisingly, Amelia is an unrelated Germanic name with no special significance to Christianity.

Significance: Emilia was a 4th century Greek woman who was the mother of Saint Basil and four other saints.

Popularity: top 500 ↑

Related names:

Emiliana – uncommon ↑

Spelling variations: *Emelia*

Emily

Origin: diminutive of Emilia.

Significance: see Emilia.

Popularity: top 10 ↓

Related names:

Emilyn – endangered ↑

Helena

Origin: elaboration of Helen, Greek meaning "light."

Significance: Helena was a 3rd century Roman empress and mother of Constantine I. Her influence on her son was vastly important to the spread of Christianity because Constantine I became the first Christian Roman emperor, and he did much to support and promote the religion.

Popularity: top 1000 →

Cross-reference: Helen is the name of a Christian martyr and is listed, with her many variations, in chapter 4, "Early Martyrs" (page 70).

Hillary

Origin: Latin meaning "cheerful."

Significance: Hilarius was pope from 461-468, during which time he worked to strengthen the church and the papacy.

Popularity: once a unisex name, with *Hillary* as the usual spelling for girls and *Hilary* as the usual spelling for boys. In the US it is now used exclusively for girls – uncommon ↓

Related names:

Ellery – Celtic form of Hilary. It has traditionally been a boys' name, but now it is given almost exclusively to girls. – uncommon ↑

Leona

Origin: feminine of Leon, the (older) Greek form of Leo, meaning "lion."

Significance: Leo was the name of thirteen popes, the first being Saint Leo the Great who was pope from 440-461.

Popularity: top 1000 ↑

Related names:

Leonie – endangered ↑

Leonela – endangered →

Marcella

Origin: feminine of Marcellus, which is a diminutive of Marcus.

Significance: Marcella was a wealthy Roman woman of the 4th century who, being widowed at a young age, dedicated her life and fortune to helping the needy. She was an early influence on Christian traditions that would develop into religious orders.

Popularity: uncommon ↓

Melanie

Origin: short form of Melania, Greek meaning "black."

Significance: There were two saints named Melania, a grandmother and granddaughter, both of whom were ascetic Christians of Rome. Melania the younger, in particular, was known for her charity and the establishment of various religious buildings.

Popularity: top 100 →

Related names:

Melania – endangered →

Spelling variations: *Melany*

Monica

Origin: North African name whose meaning has been lost.

Significance: Monica lived in North Africa in the 4th century. She was the mother of St. Augustine, and was a pious and influential woman who is venerated as a saint in her own right.

Popularity: top 1000 ↓

Related names:

Monique – French – uncommon ↓

Nicole

Origin: feminine of Nicholas, Greek meaning "victory of the people."

Significance: Nicholas was a 4th century Greek bishop during the reign of Constantine I, a time of active efforts to unify the church. He was, of course, known for secretly giving gifts to those in need.

Popularity: top 500 ↓

Related names:

Nikki – diminutive – uncommon ↓

Nicola – traditionally a Slavic boys' name. In the US, it is also used for girls, but is very rare for both boys and girls – ♂♀ endangered ↓

Patricia

Origin: feminine of Patrick, Latin meaning "patrician."

Significance: Patrick was a 5th century Romano-British missionary who was an important figure in the Christianization of Ireland. He is a patron saint of that island nation.

Popularity: top 1000 ↓

Related names:

Trisha – short form of Patricia – uncommon ↓

Patty – diminutive of Patricia – endangered ↓

Patsy – diminutive of Patty, on the same pattern as Betsy from Betty and itsy-bitsy from itty-bitty – endangered ↓

Patrice – French masculine of Patrick, used as a feminine form in the US – endangered ↓

Saints of the Middle Ages

Adelaide

Origin: contraction of Adelheidis, a Germanic name meaning "noble type."

Significance: Holy Roman empress from 962-973.

Popularity: top 500 ↑

Related names:

Adelaida – endangered →

Alexis

Origin: Greek meaning "protector, defender."

Significance: a noble Roman of the Eastern Roman Empire. He left his home and family on the day of his wedding to live a life of poverty and penance.

Popularity: ♂♀ top 100 ↓

Related names:

Alexia – feminine – top 500 ↓

Alessia – Italian – uncommon ↑

Alex – short form – ♂ uncommon →

Alexi – short form – endangered ↓

Alexius – Latin – endangered ↓

Alika – Hawaiian – endangered →

Alice

Origin: contraction of Adelis, which is a contraction of Adelheidis.

Significance: see Adelaide.

Popularity: top 100 ↑

Alicia

Origin: Latin form of Alice. It is traditionally pronounced ah-LISS-ee-ah, but the more common pronunciation in the US is now uh-LEESH-uh.

Significance: see Adelaide.

Popularity: top 500 ↓

Spelling variations: *Alisha*

Allie

Origin: short form of both Alexis and Allison.

Significance: see Alexis and Adelaide.

Popularity: top 500 ↓

Spelling variations: *Ally*

Cross-reference: Because Allie is also a short form of Alexandra, the name is included in chapter 4, "Early Martyrs" (page 66).

Allison

Origin: English last name meaning "Alice's son." Patronymic last names (based on the father's name) are quite common, but matronymic last names like Allison (based on the mother's name) are fairly rare.

Significance: see Adelaide.

Popularity: top 100 →

Spelling variations: *Alison, Allyson, Alyson, Alisson*

Alyssa

Origin: variation of Alicia.

Significance: see Adelaide.

Popularity: top 100 ↓

Spelling variations: *Alissa, Alisa*

Annabelle

Origin: variation of Amabel, a medieval French name from the Latin name Amabilis, meaning "loveable."

Significance: Amabel comes from Amabilis. See Mabel.

Popularity: top 100 ↑

Related names:

Annabella – top 500 ↑

Annebelle – endangered ↑

Spelling variations: *Annabel, Annabell*

Antonia

Origin: both the name of an ancient Roman family and its feminine form.

Significance: Saint Anthony was a 13th century Portuguese priest who spent years living an ascetic life in the desert. He inspired many to follow his example and is therefore considered the "father of monasticism."

Popularity: top 1000 ↑

Related names:

Antonella – uncommon ↑

Toni – much more popular for boys, though the spelling *Toni* is used almost exclusively for girls. – ♂ uncommon ↓

Nella – endangered ↑

Antonina – endangered →

Antoinette – endangered ↓

Anthony – ♂ endangered ↓

Arabella

Origin: Scottish variation of Annabelle.

Significance: ultimately from Amabilis. See Mabel.

Popularity: top 500 ↑

Related names:

Arabelle – uncommon ↑

Ayden

Origin: variant spelling of Aidan, the English form of the Gaelic name Aodhan. Aodhan is a diminutive of Aodh, Celtic meaning "fire."

Significance: in the 7th century, an Irish monk and missionary. After the fall of the Roman Empire, England generally fell back into paganism. Aiden helped to re-establish Christianity.

Popularity: ♂ endangered ↓

Azelie

Origin: French meaning "azalea."

Significance: Azelie was the mother of Saint Theresa of Jesus.

Popularity: endangered →

Related names:

Zelie – endangered →

Beckett

Origin: traditionally a last name. It has two separate origins. 1) diminutive of a word related to beak, for someone with a big nose. 2) last name for someone who lived at a bee cot—a cottage in the Middle Ages was a small, single-family farm.

Significance: Thomas Becket was an archbishop of Canterbury who resisted the efforts of King Henry II to weaken the relationship between the English church and Rome, leading to his assassination and status as a martyr of his faith.

Popularity: ♂ endangered ↑

Bennett

Origin: diminutive of Benedict, Latin meaning "blessed." It has traditionally been used as a last name.

Significance: in the 6th century, Saint Benedict founded many communities for monks in Italy and established rules for their behavior.

Popularity: ♂ uncommon ↑

Brenda

Origin: feminine of Brendan, a form of the Irish name Bréanainn, from a Welsh word meaning "prince."

Significance: a 6th century Irish monk who founded several monasteries. He was a famous navigator, particularly known for his legendary voyage to Isle of the Blessed, a phantom island in the North Atlantic Ocean.

Popularity: top 1000 ↓

Related names:

Brenna – top 1000 ↓

Bridget

Origin: English form of Brigid, Celtic meaning "exalted one."

Significance: there are two saints named Bridget: 1) The earliest (c. 451-525) is one of Ireland's three patron saints. She was a nun and religious leader who founded several convents in Ireland. 2) The later Saint Bridget (1303-1373) is the patron saint of Sweden. Her many visions influenced forms of prayers and religious art.

Popularity: top 1000 ↑

Related names:

Bree – English nickname for Bridget – uncommon →

Bridie – English nickname for Bridget – endangered →

Britta – contraction of Birgitta, the Scandinavian form of Bridget – endangered →

Britt – short form of Britta – endangered →

Berit – short form of Berita, a variation of Scandinavian Birgitta – endangered ↓

Camila

Origin: a warrior princess of Roman mythology. Camila was also a Roman title for acolytes of the priests of Jupiter— in this sense the name was later used as a patrician Roman family name, with Camila also being the feminine form.

Significance: there are two saints named Camilla: 1) The first was a 5th century hermitess. 2) The second was a 15th century Italian princess who became increasingly devout throughout her childhood until she finally gave up court life at the age of 23 to become a nun.

Popularity: top 100 ↑

Related names:

Camille – top 500 →

Spelling variations: *Camilla*

Carly

Origin: feminine diminutive of Carl.

Significance: see Charlie.

Popularity: top 500 ↓

Spelling variations: *Karlee, Carlee, Karlie, Carlie*

Caroline

Origin: feminine diminutive of Carl.

Significance: see Charlie.

Popularity: top 100 →

Related names:

Carolina – elaboration – top 500 ↓

Carolyn – diminutive – top 1000 ↓

Carrie – diminutive of Caroline and other related names – uncommon ↓

Carol – feminine form of Carl – uncommon ↓

Arie – short form of Carrie and Mary – endangered ↑

Cross-reference: Carol is also listed in chapter 2 (page 37).

Chantal

Origin: Provençal place name meaning "rock, boulder."

Significance: Chantal is given in honor of Saint Jane Frances de Chantal (1572-1641). The wealthy and widowed Baroness de Chantal founded the Order of the Visitation of Holy Mary to visit and care for the poor and sick. The order was unusual in that the sisters were not cloistered but went out among the people.

Popularity: endangered ↓

Charlie

Origin: diminutive of Charles, the French form of the Germanic name Carl. The name means "man" and has the connotation "common man" or "freeman."

Significance: there have been many saints named Charles (or one of the several variations of the name): the earliest and best-known of these saints is Charlemagne, the first Holy Roman emperor.

Popularity: traditionally a boys' name, it is now nearly as popular for girls as it is for boys– ♂♀ top 500 ↑

Related names:

Charlene – feminine of Charles – uncommon →

Charlize – South African – uncommon ↓

Charles – French form of Carl – ♂ endangered →

Spelling variations: *Charlee, Charley, Charleigh, Charli*

Charlotte

Origin: feminine diminutive of Charles, the French form of Carl.

Significance: see Charlie.

Popularity: top 10 ↑

Related names:

Lottie – diminutive – endangered ↑

Carlota – Iberian – endangered →

Arlette – short form – uncommon →

Arleth – Spanish variation of Arlette – uncommon ↓

Claire

Origin: from Latin *clarus* meaning "clear" and, by extension, "bright" and later "famous."

Significance: Saint Clare of Assisi (1194-1253) was an Italian nun and, with Saint Francis of Assisi, a founder of the Poor Clares, a religious order.

Popularity: top 100 →

Related names:

Clara – top 500 ↑

Clarissa – top 500 ↓

Clarice – endangered →

Clarita – endangered →

Clarabelle – endangered →

Spelling variations: *Clare*

Claudia

Origin: both the name of an imperial Roman family and its feminine form.

Significance: Claudius of Besançon was a 7th century French bishop.

Popularity: top 1000 ↓

Daylin

Origin: variant spelling of Dallan, Irish Gaelic meaning "little blind one." It was a nickname given to Dallan Forgaill because he so damaged his eyesight by constant studying.

Significance: Dallan Forgaill was an Irish scholar and poet, particularly known for his eulogies of Irish saints.

Popularity: ♂ endangered →

Dominique

Origin: French feminine of Dominic, from *dies Dominica*, Latin for "day of the Lord," Sunday. The name was often given to children born on Sunday.

Significance: Saint Dominic was a Spanish priest who, in 1215, founded the Dominican Order, an intellectual order dedicated to learning and teaching.

Popularity: uncommon ↓

Related names:

Dominica – Italian – endangered →

Elodie

Origin: French form of Alodia.

Significance: Alodia was a Spanish child who, with her sister Nunilo, was martyred by the Muslims during the Moorish occupation of Spain.

Popularity: uncommon ↑

Emma

Origin: short form of Germanic names starting with *irm/erm*, from *erman*, meaning "whole." Examples included Irmalinda, "wholly tender" and Ermintrude, "wholly strong."

Significance: there were two saints named Emma: the Austrian Emma of Gurk (980-1045) and the German Emma of Lesum (c. 975-1038). Both saints have a similar history—they were rich women of noble families who founded many churches and supported charitable work, such as care for the sick and poor.

Popularity: top 10 →

Related names:

Emmagrace – endangered ↑

Emmarose – endangered ↑

Emmarae – endangered ↑

Emmalia – endangered →

Emmajean – endangered →

Emmalise – endangered →

Emmakate – endangered →

Emmaline

Origin: diminutive of Emma.

Significance: see Emma.

Popularity: top 1000 ↑

Related names:

Emmalina – endangered →

Spelling variations: *Emmeline*

Emmalyn

Origin: diminutive of Emma.

Significance: see Emma.

Popularity: top 500 ↑

Related names:

Emmalene – endangered →

Spelling variations: *Emmalynn*

Emmy

Origin: diminutive of Emma.

Significance: See Emma.

Popularity: top 1000 ↑

Related names:

Emmylou – endangered ↑

Frances

Origin: feminine spelling of Francis, a short form of Francesco, which is Italian meaning "Frenchman." It was a nickname for Saint Francis of Assisi, given to him by his father, who was in France on business when his son was born. The saint's given name was Giovanni.

Significance: though never ordained a priest, Saint Francis was an effective preacher and missionary who founded three religious orders, including the extraordinarily influential Third Order of St. Francis.

Popularity: ♂♀ top 1000 →

Related names:

Frankie – diminutive of Frank, a masculine short form of Francis – ♂ uncommon ↑

Fanny – endangered →

Francesca

Origin: feminine of Francesco. See Frances.

Significance: see Frances.

Popularity: top 500 →

Related names:

Francine – variation of Françoise, the French form of Francesca – endangered →

Genevieve

Origin: Celtic name whose meaning is unknown. The most likely meaning is "born noble." Many sources claim it is a Germanic name meaning "tribal woman," but this is an unlikely etymology.

Significance: a patron saint of Paris. She is believed to have saved the city from the Huns in 451. Genevieve convinced the Parisians to stay in the city and pray for salvation, after which Attila invaded Orleans rather than Paris.

Popularity: top 500 ↑

Georgia

Origin: feminine of George, Greek meaning "farmer."

Significance: Georgia was a 5th century French nun who lived a life of solitude and prayer.

Popularity: top 500 ↑

Related names:

Georgina – Germanic feminine – uncommon →

Gina – Italian diminutive of names ending with –gina – uncommon ↓

Georgie – English diminutive – endangered →

Georgette – French feminine – endangered →

Georgiana – English feminine – endangered ↑

Gigi – French diminutive of Georgine – endangered →

Cross-reference: Because Georgia is also given in honor of Saint George, the patron saint of England, it is listed in chapter 4, "Early Martyrs" (page 70).

Gertrude

Origin: Germanic meaning "strong spear."

Significance: Gertrude the Great was a Benedictine nun in 13th century Germany. She began having visions when she was twenty-five years old, after which she dedicated herself to prayer and meditation, and to spiritual study and writing. The most influential of her writings, *The Herald of Divine Love*, is still read today.

Popularity: endangered →

Related names:

Trudy – endangered →

Greer

Origin: Scottish form of Gregory, ultimately Greek meaning "watchful, alert." Originally a last name.

Significance: Pope Gregory I is considered "the father of Christian worship" for the many changes he made to the traditional forms and order of the liturgy. The established form of chants, for example, are attributed to him and were named for him—the Gregorian chants.

Popularity: endangered ↑

Heidi

Origin: short form of Adelheidis, a Germanic name meaning "noble type."

Significance: see Adelaide.

Popularity: top 500 →

Henrietta

Origin: feminine of Henry, Germanic meaning "home ruler."

Significance: there were three saints named Henry: 1) Henry II who was Holy Roman emperor from 1014-1024; 2) a 12th century English bishop who is believed to have been a missionary to Finland; 3) Henry of Cocket, a 12th century Danish hermit.

Popularity: endangered ↑

Related names:

Etta – uncommon ↑

Joan

Origin: the oldest English feminine of John, Hebrew meaning "He has favored."

Significance: Joan of Arc was a young French woman who, inspired by visions of saints, helped bring an end to the Hundred Years' War. She fought in battle for the restoration of Charles VII to the French throne and was ultimately burned at the stake by the English.

Popularity: ♂ endangered →

Related names:

Joni – endangered →

Cross-reference: Joan, as a form of John, is also a Biblical name and is listed in chapter 2 (page 40).

Joyce

Origin: ultimately from Judoc, a Celtic name meaning "lord."

Significance: Saint Judoc was a 7th century prince of Brittany (now north-western France) who gave up his throne for the priesthood. He made a pilgrimage to Rome and later lived as a hermit.

Popularity: a masculine name in France but used exclusively for girls in the US – top 1000 →

Karla

Origin: feminine of Carl.

Significance: see Charlie.

Popularity: top 1000 ↓

Spelling variations: *Carla*

Keira

Origin: Keira is an English spelling of Ciara, the feminine of the Celtic name Ciaran, meaning "dark." The letter *k* is not used in the Irish alphabet.

Significance: there have been twenty-six Irish saints named Ciaran: The earliest was Ciaran of Saigir (501-530), an Irish nobleman and bishop who founded a monastery in central Ireland.

Popularity: top 500 ↓

Spelling variations: *Kira, Kiara, Kyra, Kiera, Ciara*

Kelis

Origin: combination of Kenneth and Eveliss, the names of musician Kelis Rogers' parents. Eveliss appears to be a diminutive of Eve.

Significance: there have been two saints named Kenneth: 1) Cainnech of Aghaboe, a 6th century Irish missionary who founded numerous monasteries; 2) Saint Cenydd, a 6th century Welsh hermit. Eve was the first woman, created by God as a companion for Adam.

Popularity: uncommon →

Landry

Origin: from the Germanic name Landric, meaning "land-power."

Significance: Landry was the name of two French bishops of the early Middle Ages.

Popularity: top 1000 ↑

Laura

Origin: short form of Laurel, a fragrant evergreen. In antiquity laurel branches were woven into crowns worn as symbols of victory.

Significance: Saint Laura was a Spanish abbess who was martyred by Muslims during the Moorish occupation.

Popularity: top 500 ↓

Related names:

    Loretta – uncommon ↑

    Alora – uncommon →

    Laurie – endangered →

Lexi

Origin: short form of Alexis, Greek meaning "protector, defender."

Significance: see Alexis.

Popularity: top 500 ↑

Related names:

    Lexa – English – endangered →

    Lexia – English – endangered ↓

    Lexis – English – endangered ↓

Spelling variations: *Lexie*

Cross-reference: Lexi is also listed in chapter 4, "Early Martyrs" (page 73).

Lyra

Origin: the name of a place in Normandy.

Significance: Nicholas of Lyra (1270-1349) was a Jewish convert who became a Franciscan monk. He was a great scholar whose knowledge of Hebrew and Jewish commentary strongly influenced his book of Biblical commentary, the first such work to be printed and a greatly influential text for some centuries.

Popularity: uncommon ↑

Mabel

Origin: English short form of the medieval French name Amabel, from the Latin name Amabilis, meaning "loveable."

Significance: there have been two saints named Amabilis: 1) The earliest was 5th century French priest. 2) The second saint named Amabilis, called Saint Mabel, was a 7th century English princess who became a nun in France.

Popularity: endangered ↑

Mandy

Origin: diminutive of Amanda, which is a feminine of Amandus, Latin meaning "worthy of love."

Significance: there were two saints named Amandus, both of whom were French bishops. One lived in the 5th and the other in the 7th century.

Popularity: uncommon ↓

Related names:

Amanda – endangered ↓

Olga

Origin: Germanic meaning "blessed."

Significance: in the 10th century, Olga became the first Christian ruler in Eastern Europe, acting as regent for her son. Upon seeing the church Saint Sophia in Constantinople (now Istanbul), she converted to Christianity, believing that such magnificent and beautiful place must truly be the house of God. Olga's grandson, whom she instructed in her faith, ultimately made Christianity the official religion of the state.

Popularity: endangered ↓

Olympia

Origin: the mountain home of the Greek gods.

Significance: a wealthy widow of 4th century Constantinople (now Istanbul) who used her fortune to help the poor and sick. She was a deaconess and was active in church politics.

Popularity: endangered ↑

Remi

Origin: short form of Remigius, Latin meaning "oarsman."

Significance: Saint Remigius was a French bishop who baptized Clovis, the first king of all the Franks, on Christmas day in 496. Clovis's conversion eventually led all of France to become Catholic. Clovis was converted by his wife, Clotilde, who was a close friend of Saint Genevieve.

Popularity: this name is also used for boys, with the spelling *Remy* – ♂♀ top 1000 ↑

Spelling variations: *Remy*

Rita

Origin: short form of Margarita, the Latin transliteration of the Greek word *margarites*, meaning "pearl."

Significance: Rita of Cascia (1381-1457) was a gentle and pious Italian woman who lived a hard life in a violent time and place among a family of violent men. She patiently worked to improve their characters, and, though she could not save her husband and children, she ultimately ended a long and bloody feud involving her husband's family. After this she was allowed to enter a convent where she lived peacefully until her death.

Popularity: uncommon →

Cross-reference: Rita is also listed in chapter 4, "Early Martyrs" (page 74).

Ronnie

Origin: diminutive of Ronald, Germanic meaning "rules with council."

Significance: Saint Ronald (Rognvald Kale Kolsson) was a Norwegian earl of the Orkney Islands (now a part of Scotland) who had a great cathedral built there. He is particularly well-known for a pilgrimage to the Holy Land.

Popularity: endangered →

Cross-reference: Ronnie is also a diminutive of Veronica, which is listed in the section titled "Christian Concepts" in chapter 3 (page 55).

Rosalie

Origin: short form of Rosalia, which is a variation of Rosa, Latin meaning "rose."

Significance: Rosalia was a noble woman who lived as a hermitess near Palermo, Sicily, where she is the patron saint. Her spirit is believed to have saved the city from a plague nearly 500 years after her death.

Popularity: top 500 ↑

Related names:

Rosalia – uncommon ↑

Rowan

Origin: English spelling of Ruadhan, Gaelic meaning "little red."

Significance: Ruadhan of Lorrha was a 6th century Irish prophet who founded a monastery, of which he was the abbot, in central Ireland.

Popularity: top 500 ↑

Solange

Origin: variation of the Latin name Sollemnia, meaning "solemn."

Significance: Solange was a shepherdess of 9th century Provence renown for her piety and purity. She died (c. 880) defending her virginity against an aristocrat whose marriage proposal she had refused.

Popularity: endangered →

Willa

Origin: feminine short form of William, Germanic meaning "intending to protect."

Significance: there have been thirty-five saints name William, the earliest of whom was William of Gellone, a French count and military leader who protected France against the invading Moors. In 804 he founded a monastery where he lived as a monk until his death.

Popularity: top 1000 ↑

Related names:

Willamina – also a feminine of William – endangered ↑

Mena – short form of Willamina and Philomena – endangered →

Winnie

Origin: diminutive of Winifred, Celtic meaning "peace friend."

Significance: Winifred was a 7th century Welsh noblewoman who gave up her position and wealth for the convent and eventually became an abbess.

Popularity: uncommon ↑

Related names:

Winifred – endangered ↑

Yvette

Origin: diminutive and feminine form of Yves, the French form of Ivo, which is a short form of Germanic names staring with *iv*, meaning "yew tree."

Significance: there have been three saints named Ivo: 1) The earliest, also called Saint Ives, was an 11th century English bishop who lived in Cornwall. 2) Saint Ivo of Chartre was an 11th century French bishop. 3) Saint Ivo of Kermartin was a 12th century French priest who is much-loved for having been a defender of the poor and sick.

Popularity: uncommon ↓

Related names:

Yvonne – medieval – uncommon ↓

Iva – feminine of Ivo – endangered ↑

Later Saints

Bernadette

Origin: feminine of Bernard, Germanic meaning "hardy as a bear."

Significance: Bernadette was a nickname for Marie Bernarde Soubirous (1844-1879), a shepherdess who, when she was fourteen years old, had multiple visions of the Virgin at Lourdes, a town in France.

Popularity: uncommon →

Cross-reference: The name Lourdes comes from the place where Bernadette had her visions and is listed in chapter 2 (page 33).

Edith

Origin: Germanic meaning "rich in war."

Significance: Edith Stein (1891-1942) was born into a German Jewish family. She converted to Catholicism and became a Carmelite nun after taking a PhD in philosophy.

Nevertheless, the Nazis sent her to Auschwitz with her sister, who had also converted, and both were killed.

Popularity: top 1000 →

Related names:

Edie – diminutive– uncommon ↑

Kateri

Origin: Mohawk Indian form of Katherine.

Significance: Kateri Tekakwitha (1656-1680) was a Mohawk woman who converted to Christianity despite the passionate objections of her tribe and the harassment they subjected her to. She eventually left her tribe and lived a religious life in a Jesuit mission village.

Popularity: endangered →

Cross-reference: Katherine is the name of a well-known martyr and is also listed in chapter 4 (page 72).

Louisa

Origin: feminine of Louis, Germanic meaning "famous fighter."

Significance: Louise de Marillac (1591-1660) was a co-founder of The Daughters of Charity, a religious society that organized young French noblewomen in helping the poor.

Popularity: top 1000 ↑

Related names:

Louise – uncommon ↑

Luella – diminutive – uncommon ↑

Lula – Brazilian – endangered →

Lilou – French combination of Lili and Louise; Lili is a diminutive of Elizabeth – endangered ↑

Emmylou – English combination or Emmy and Louse; Emmy is a diminutive of Emma – endangered ↑

Maite (my-TEH)

Origin: Basque contraction of Maria Teresa.

Significance: see Teresa.

Popularity: uncommon →

Cross-reference: Maite is also listed with the Mary names (page 35). And because Maite can also be a contraction of Maria Esther, it is listed with the Old Testament names (page 18).

Rose

Origin: the name of the famously beautiful and fragrant flower.

Significance: Rose of Lima (1586-1617) was the first person born in the New World to be made a saint by the Catholic Church. From childhood she was determined to dedicate herself to God. Because her family wouldn't let her take orders, she joined the Franciscans as a lay person.

Popularity: top 500 ↑

Related names:

Rosie – diminutive – top 1000 ↑

Teresa

Origin: possibly Greek meaning "harvest."

Significance: there have been ten saints named Teresa. The two best-known are: 1) Saint Teresa of Jesus (1515-1582) was a Spanish nun of the Carmelite order, a celebrated writer on the transformation of the self, and an energetic reformer. 2) Thérèse of Lisieux (1873-1897) was a French nun who is loved for her simple spirituality, expressed in many written works, particularly *The Story of a Soul.*

Popularity: top 1000 ↓

Related names:

Terri – diminutive – endangered ↓

Tessa

Origin: contraction of Teresa, which may be Greek meaning "harvest."

Significance: see Teresa.

Popularity: top 500 →

Related names:

Tess – short form – uncommon ↓

Virginia

Origin: from Verginia, which is both an ancient Roman family name and its feminine form. The name comes from a legend about a father who killed his daughter to save her from the advances of a powerful and cruel man.

Significance: Virginia Centurione Bracelli (1587-1651) was an Italian noblewoman who, having been widowed at the age of 20, dedicated her life to helping the poor and sick. Among other accomplishments, she organized a center that cared for many hundreds of people, including victims of plague.

Popularity: top 1000 →

Related names:

Ginny – English diminutive of Virginia – endangered →

Gigi – diminutive of French Verginie – endangered →

BOYS' NAMES

All of the names listed in this book are
currently used in the US. The popularity
and trending information provided for the
names is based on information released
each May by the US Social Security
Administration.

Chapter 6: The Old Testament

Genesis and Job

Abdiel

Origin: Hebrew meaning "servant of God."

Significance: mentioned in a genealogy of Reuben in 1 Chronicles.

Popularity: top 1000 ↑

Abel

Origin: Hebrew meaning "vapor."

Significance: the second son of Adam and Eve.

Popularity: top 500 ↑

Abraham

Origin: Hebrew meaning "father of multitudes." It is the name given to Abraham by God—previously he had been called Abram.

Significance: God promised Abraham many descendants and a great land for them in return for obedience.

Popularity: top 500 ↑

Related names:

Abe – short form – endangered →

Abram

Origin: Abraham's original name. Hebrew meaning "exalted father."

Significance: see Abraham.

Popularity: top 500 ↑

Related names:

Bram – short form– endangered →

Adam

Origin: Hebrew meaning "earth."

Significance: the first man, created by God.

Popularity: top 100 →

Related names:

Adán – Spanish form – top 500 ↓

Asher

Origin: Hebrew meaning "blessed, fortunate."

Significance: Jacob's son with Zilpah, Rebecca's handmaiden. A founder of one of the twelve tribes of Israel.

Popularity: top 100 ↑

Benjamin

Origin: Hebrew meaning "right-hand son."

Significance: Jacob's youngest son, with Rebecca. He was the only one who remained loyal to Joseph in the face of their brothers' jealousy.

Popularity: top 100 →

Related names:

Ben – top 1000 →

Benny – uncommon →

Benji – endangered ↑

Cain

Origin: Hebrew meaning "to acquire."

Significance: the first-born son of Adam and Eve.

Popularity: top 1000 ↑

Canaan

Origin: Hebrew name for a large region of the Middle East.

Significance: the land promised by God to the descendants of Abraham.

Popularity: uncommon ↑

Dan

Origin: Hebrew meaning "judgment."

Significance: a son of Jacob with Bilhah, one of Rachel's handmaidens. He is a founder of one of the twelve tribes of Israel.

Popularity: uncommon ↓

Eden

Origin: from Hebrew *Gan 'Edhen*, meaning "garden of God."

Significance: the paradisiacal wilderness where Adam and Eve first lived.

Popularity: ♂ top 1000 ↑

Elam

Origin: Hebrew meaning "hidden time, eternity."

Significance: the name of two places and up to seven men in the Bible. The first of the men mentioned is a son of Shem, thus a grandson of Noah.

Popularity: endangered ↑

Enoch

Origin: Hebrew meaning "teaching."

Significance: in the genealogy between Adam and Noah, Enoch is of the sixth generation after Adam (Genesis 5:21-24).

Popularity: top 1000 ↑

Enos

Origin: Hebrew meaning "mortal, frail."

Significance: in the genealogy between Adam and Noah, Enos is of the second generation after Adam (1 Chronicles 1:1).

Popularity: endangered →

Ephraim

Origin: Hebrew meaning "fruitful."

Significance: the youngest of Joseph's two sons. He is the founder of one of the twelve tribes of Israel.

Popularity: top 1000 ↑

Related names:

Efraín – Spanish – top 1000 ↓

Esau

Origin: Hebrew meaning "doer," implying a man of action.

Significance: Jacob and Esau were twin sons born to Isaac and Rebecca. Esau was the elder son, who sold his birthright to Jacob.

Popularity: endangered ↓

Genesis

Origin: Greek meaning "creation."

Significance: the name of the first book of the Bible. It's a Greek translation of the first word in the Bible, *breshit*, Hebrew meaning "in the beginning."

Popularity: ♀ endangered →

Isaac

Origin: Hebrew meaning "he laughs."

Significance: the only son of Abraham and Sarah. His name is a reminder that his parents laughed when God told them that Sarah would bear a child—both parents were very old and Sarah was well past child-bearing age.

Popularity: top 100 →

Related names:

Ike – English contraction – endangered ↑

Spelling variations: *Issac*

Ishmael

Origin: Hebrew meaning "God will listen."

Significance: the son of Abraham with his wife's Egyptian handmaiden, Hagar. After Sarah bore her own son, Hagar took Ishmael away. He had twelve sons of his own and is a patriarch and prophet of Islam.

Popularity: uncommon →

Israel

Origin: a Hebrew name, the meaning of which is uncertain. It is often thought to mean "struggles with God," "prince of God," or "governor through God."

Significance: another name for Jacob, given to him by God. As a body, Jacob's descendants were called Israelites.

Popularity: top 500 →

Jacob

Origin: Hebrew meaning "supplanter."

Significance: Jacob and Esau were twin sons born to Isaac and Rebecca. Jacob's descendants are traditionally divided into the twelve tribes of Israel.

Popularity: top 10 ↓

Related names:

Jacoby – traditionally a last name – top 1000 ↓

Jake – short form – top 500 ↓

Jacobo – Spanish – endangered →

Giacomo – Italian – endangered →

Spelling variations: *Jakob, Jaycob, Jakobe*

Cross-reference: Hebrew Ya'aqob is also the origin of James and its several variations. They are listed in chapter 7, "The New Testament" (page 111).

Jared

Origin: Hebrew meaning "descent."

Significance: in the genealogy between Adam and Noah, Jared is of the fifth generation after Adam (Genesis 5:18).

Popularity: top 500 ↓

Job

Origin: Hebrew meaning "persecuted."

Significance: a pious and prosperous man whom God allowed Satan to test. Satan inflicted great suffering on Job, but Job never lost his faith in God, who ultimately restored his former prosperity.

Popularity: endangered →

Joseph

Origin: Hebrew meaning "God will add," implying the addition of children to a family.

Significance: Jacob's favorite son, with Rebecca. He was sold by his brothers as a slave in Egypt, where he became a powerful man and ultimately was able to save all his family during a long period of famine.

Popularity: top 100 ↓

Related names:

José – Iberian – top 100 ↓

Joe – short form – top 1000 ↓

Joey – diminutive – top 1000 ↓

Giuseppe – Italian – uncommon →

Jody – ♂♀ endangered →

Cross-reference: Joseph is also listed in chapter 7 (page 112).

Judah

Origin: Hebrew meaning "praised."

Significance: a son of Jacob and Leah. He was the founder of one of the twelve tribes of Israel.

Popularity: top 500 ↑

Cross-reference: Because Judah was also the name of the southern kingdom of Israel, it is listed a second time in this chapter, in the section titled "The Kingdom of Israel" (page 104).

Kenan

Origin: Hebrew meaning "sorrow."

Significance: in the genealogy between Adam and Noah, Kenan is of the third generation after Adam (1 Chronicles 1:1-3).

Popularity: uncommon →

Levi

Origin: Hebrew meaning "attached."

Significance: Jacob's third son, with Leah. The Levites became priests and went to live among the other tribes.

Popularity: top 100 ↑

Manasseh

Origin: Hebrew meaning "causing to forget."

Significance: the oldest of Joseph's two sons. He is the founder of one of the twelve tribes of Israel.

Popularity: endangered →

Noah

Origin: Hebrew meaning "rest" or "comfort."

Significance: God sent a great flood to destroy all of mankind because the people's behavior was wicked. He chose Noah to save all the animals who lived on dry land and his own family, making all people living today Noah's descendants.

Popularity: top 10 ↑

Related names:

Noe (NOW) – a variation used in several languages – top 1000 →

Ruben

Origin: Hebrew meaning "behold, a son."

Significance: Jacob's first son, with Leah. He is the founder of one of the twelve tribes of Israel.

Popularity: top 500 ↓

Spelling variations: *Reuben*

Seth

Origin: Hebrew meaning "placed, appointed."

Significance: Adam and Eve's third son, born after Abel's death.

Popularity: top 500 ↓

Simon

Origin: Hebrew meaning "to hear" or "to be heard."

Significance: Jacob's second son, with Leah. He is the founder of one of the twelve tribes of Israel.

Popularity: top 500 →

Related names:

Simeon – uncommon →

Zebulon

Origin: Hebrew of uncertain meaning.

Significance: Jacob's tenth son, and the youngest of the sons born to Leah.

Popularity: endangered →

Exodus and Early Years in Canaan

Aaron

Origin: possibly an ancient Egyptian name, but its meaning is not known.

Significance: a priest and a leader of the Israelites. He was Moses's brother and spoke to the people for Moses, who had a speech impediment.

Popularity: top 100 →

Spelling variations: *Aron*

Cross-reference: Aaron is also the name of an early martyr. See chapter 9 for more information (page 129).

Caleb

Origin: Hebrew meaning "whole-hearted."

Significance: a spy sent by Moses to Canaan to see if it were possible to conquer the land.

Popularity: top 100 ↓

Spelling variations: *Kaleb*

Canaan

Origin: the Hebrew name for a large region of the Middle East.

Significance: the land promised by God to the descendants of Abraham.

Popularity: uncommon ↑

Cohen

Origin: Hebrew meaning "priest."

Significance: the Cohen are the descendants of Aaron, who fulfill priestly duties within Judaism.

Popularity: top 500 ↑

Spelling variations: *Kohen*

Eliezer

Origin: Hebrew meaning "God has helped."

Significance: Aaron's son and the second high priest, after his father.

Popularity: top 1000 →

Exodus

Origin: Greek meaning "going out."

Significance: the name of the second book of the Bible. It tells how the Israelites left slavery in Egypt and how they received the Ten Commandments.

Popularity: endangered →

Gadiel

Origin: variant spelling of Gaddiel, Hebrew meaning "fortune is God."

Significance: a leader of the tribe of Zebulun and one of twelve men sent by Moses to explore Canaan.

Popularity: endangered →

Gideon

Origin: Hebrew meaning "feller of trees."

Significance: a judge and a prophet who spoke out against the worship of the Canaanite gods. He led a small force of Israelites to victory over a much large force of Canaanites.

Popularity: top 500 ↑

Jairo (HYE-ro)

Origin: Spanish form of Jair, Hebrew meaning "He illuminates."

Significance: see Yahir.

Popularity: top 1000 ↓

Jericho

Origin: a Canaanite word meaning "fragrant."

Significance: the first city conquered by the Israelites after they entered Canaan. The city walls miraculously crumbled as Israelite soldiers marched around the city blowing horns. However, Jericho became an accursed city: every person and animal in it was killed and the city itself was burned.

Popularity: top 1000 ↑

Joshua

Origin: Hebrew meaning "Yahweh is salvation."

Significance: led the Israelites into the land of Canaan after the death of Moses.

Popularity: top 100 ↓

Related names:

Josue – used in several Romance languages – top 500 ↓

Josh – short form – uncommon ↓

Jeshua – used in the Bible as a variation of Joshua, as in Nehemiah 8:17. Jeshua is a short form of Yehoshua, the Hebrew form of Joshua – endangered →

Moses

Origin: possibly an ancient Egyptian name meaning "saved from the water"; or it may come from Hebrew meaning "to draw," because Moses was drawn out of the Nile River.

Significance: the most important prophet of the Old Testament. He brought the Israelites out of slavery, received the Ten Commandments from God, and led the people during their forty years in the wilderness.

Popularity: top 500 →

Related names:

Moises – Iberian – top 500 ↓

Phineas

Origin: Hebrew meaning "mouth of brass," with the connotation of "oracle."

Significance: grandson of Aaron and son of Eleazar. He was the third high priest, after his father.

Popularity: uncommon →

Samson

Origin: Hebrew meaning "sun."

Significance: a prophet who freed the Israelites from the Philistines (a people of Canaan). God gave Samson supernatural strength on the condition that he never drink alcohol or cut his hair.

Popularity: top 1000 ↑

Shiloh

Origin: Hebrew, possibly meaning "He whose it is."

Significance: a city where the Tabernacle was kept for 369 years. The Tabernacle is a tent sanctuary that was the assembly place of the Israelites and home of the Ark of the Covenant.

Popularity: traditionally a boys' name, but now more popular for girls. – ♂♀ uncommon ↑

Uziel

Origin: Hebrew meaning "God is my strength."

Significance: a grandson of Levi and uncle of Moses, Aaron, and Miriam.

Popularity: endangered →

Yael (ya-EL)

Origin: the Hebrew word for the Nubian ibex.

Significance: a Canaanite woman who sympathized with the Israelites. She killed Jabin's army commander when he came to her husband's tent for refuge after being defeated by the Israelites in battle (Judges 4:17-22).

Popularity: ♂♀ top 1000 →

Related names:

Jael (Ja-EL) – English form of Yael – uncommon →

Yahir (ya-EER)

Origin: Spanish form of Jair, Hebrew meaning "He illuminates."

Significance: Yahir was a judge of the Israelites who had thirty sons.

Popularity: top 1000 ↓

Spelling variations: *Jair, Yair*

Note: Jair is more commonly used by Spanish-speakers. When used by English-speakers, it's pronounced JAY-er.

Cross-reference: Jairus, a New Testament form of Jair, is listed in chapter 7, "The New Testament" in the section titled "People and Places in the Life of Jesus" (page 111).

Zuriel

Origin: Hebrew meaning "God is a rock (of strength)."

Significance: mentioned in Numbers (3:35) as "the leader of the Merarite clan" of Levites.

Popularity: endangered ↑

The Kingdom of Israel

Abner

Origin: Hebrew meaning "father of light."

Significance: Saul's cousin and the chief commander of his army.

Popularity: uncommon ↑

Adiel

Origin: Hebrew meaning "ornament of God."

Significance: mentioned in a list of "Officials of David's Kingdom." His son, Azmaveth, "was in charge of the palace treasuries" (1 Chronicles 27:25).

Popularity: endangered →

Amos

Origin: Hebrew meaning "carried."

Significance: a prophet during a time of prosperity for both the northern Kingdom of Israel and the southern Kingdom of Judah. He was concerned with right behavior and just action.

Popularity: top 1000 ↑

Ariel

Origin: Hebrew meaning "lion of God."

Significance: a metaphorical name for Jerusalem, which David established as the capital of the united Kingdom of Israel.

Popularity: top 1000 ↓

Asa

Origin: Hebrew meaning "healer."

Significance: Asa was the third king of Judah. He led the people in right worship of God.

Popularity: top 1000 ↑

Axel

Origin: Scandinavian form of Absalom, Hebrew meaning, "father is peace."

Significance: Absolom was David's third son. He was handsome and stylish, but also deceitful and hungry for power.

Popularity: top 500 ↑

Related names:

Absalom – endangered →

Azriel

Origin: Hebrew meaning "help of God."

Significance: there are three Biblical characters named Azriel: two are mentioned in Chronicles and one is the last high priest of the united Kingdom of Israel.

Popularity: endangered →

Benaiah (ben-AI-uh)

Origin: Hebrew meaning "built up of Yahweh."

Significance: there are at least a dozen Biblical figures named Benaiah. The most well-known was one of David's greatest warriors.

Popularity: endangered ↑

Boaz

Origin: Hebrew meaning "by strength."

Significance: Ruth's second husband and an ancestor of King David through their son, Obed.

Popularity: uncommon ↑

David

Origin: Hebrew meaning "beloved."

Significance: the second king of the united Israelite tribes.

Popularity: top 100 ↓

Related names:

Dawson – an English last name meaning "Daw's son"; Daw was a medieval English form of David – top 500 ↓

Davis – Welsh short form of Davidson – top 500 →

Davi – Portuguese form of David – endangered ↑

Davey – English diminutive of David – endangered →

Kingdavid – an American blend of king and David – endangered →

Eli

Origin: Hebrew meaning "my God."

Significance: a high priest and prophet, and the mentor of Samuel, the last of the judges who led the tribes of Israel.

Popularity: top 100 ↑

Elias

Origin: the New Testament form of Elijah, Hebrew meaning "my God is Yahweh."

Significance: see Elijah.

Popularity: top 500 ↑

Elijah

Origin: Hebrew meaning "my God is Yahweh."

Significance: a prophet in the northern Kingdom of Israel. He spoke out against the worship of the Canaanite gods and performed many miracles, such as resurrecting the dead.

Popularity: top 100 →

Spelling variations: *Alijah*

Elisha

Origin: Hebrew meaning "my God is salvation."

Significance: Elijah's successor. He was a prophet of the northern Kingdom of Israel who performed many miracles and continued to warn the people not to worship the Canaanite gods.

Popularity: top 1000 →

Elliot

Origin: a diminutive of Elias, the New Testament form of Elijah.

Significance: see Elijah.

Popularity: top 500 ↑

Spelling variations: *Elliott, Eliot*

Ethan

Origin: Hebrew meaning "solid, strong," implying permanence.

Significance: mentioned in the Old Testament in comparison with Solomon, the comparison being that Ethan was a very wise man, but Solomon was even wiser (1 Kings 4:30-31). Ethan was the author of Psalm 89.

Popularity: top 10 ↓

Hezekiah

Origin: Hebrew meaning "Yahweh strengthens."

Significance: Hezekiah was one of the righteous kings of the southern Kingdom of Judah. He led the people in right worship of God and defended the kingdom against attacks from the Assyrians (a Canaanite people).

Popularity: top 1000 ↑

Hosea

Origin: Hebrew meaning "salvation."

Significance: a prophet and the author of the Book of Hosea. His prophecies deal with the sins of the people, and foretell their future destruction and ultimate forgiveness by God.

Popularity: endangered ↑

Isaiah

Origin: Hebrew meaning "Yahweh is salvation."

Significance: prophet who foretold the fall of Jerusalem as a punishment for the sins of the people, the coming of the Messiah, and the ultimate restoration of Jerusalem.

Popularity: top 100 ↓

Related names:

Isais – top 1000 →

Spelling variations: *Izaiah, Isiah, Izayah*

Jadiel (JAH-dee-el)

Origin: Hebrew meaning "God makes glad."

Significance: Jadiel is mentioned in Chronicles as the head of a household of the tribe of Manasseh.

Popularity: top 1000 ↓

Jedidiah

Origin: Hebrew meaning "friend of God."

Significance: another name for Solomon; it was given to him by God.

Popularity: top 1000 ↑

Jeremiah

Origin: Hebrew meaning "God uplifts."

Significance: Jeremiah was a prophet during the reign of Josiah. He reminded the people of their sins and foretold the destruction of Jerusalem.

Popularity: top 100 →

Related names:

Jeremy – diminutive of Jeremiah – top 500 ↓

Jerry – contraction of Jeremy – top 500 ↓

Jeremias – used in several Romance languages – uncommon ↑

Jesse (JESS-ee)

Origin: Hebrew meaning "God exists." It is derived like this: Hebrew Yishai > Greek Iessai > Latin Iesse > Late Latin Jesse.

Significance: the father of David, second king of the Israelites.

Popularity: top 500 ↓

Related names:

Jess – short form – endangered ↓

Isai – form of Jesse used in many Germanic and Romance languages. It is derived like this: Hebrew Yishai > Greek Iessai > Latin Isai – uncommon ↓

Jessejames – English combination of Jesse and James – endangered →

Spelling variations: *Jessie*

Jonah

Origin: Hebrew meaning "dove."

Significance: a prophet of the northern Kingdom of Israel who tried to flee his calling. While he was sailing away from Nineveh, the city God commanded him to enter, there was a wild storm. Jonah was thrown overboard and swallowed by a great fish who took him back to dry land. Jonah then fulfilled his duty.

Popularity: top 500 →

Related names:

Jonas – top 500 →

Jonathan

Origin: Hebrew meaning "God has given." Neither Jonathan nor the short form Jon is related to John (page 117).

Significance: Saul's son and a good friend of David.

Popularity: top 100 ↓

Related names:

Jon – top 1000 ↓

Spelling variations: *Johnathan, Jonathon, Johnathon*

Josiah

Origin: Hebrew meaning "founded of the Lord."

Significance: when the people had again begun to worship Canaanite gods, Josiah, as king, led them back to right worship. However, God had promised to destroy Jerusalem, and Josiah died fighting as the city fell to the Egyptians.

Popularity: top 100 ↑

Related names:

Jasiah – top 1000 ↑

Jesiah – uncommon →

Spelling variations: *Joziah*

Judah

Origin: Hebrew meaning "praised."

Significance: after the death of King Solomon, the Kingdom of Israel divided into two: a southern kingdom called Judah and a northern kingdom—still called the Kingdom of Israel.

Popularity: top 500 ↑

Cross-reference: Judah was also the name of a son of Jacob. For more information see the first section in this chapter, "Genesis and Job" (page 97).

Lemuel

Origin: Hebrew meaning "belonging to God."

Significance: a king who is mentioned in Proverbs. "The sayings of King Lemuel" warn that kings should not drink alcohol and that they must stand up for the weak and vulnerable.

Popularity: endangered →

Micah (MY-kuh)

Origin: from the same root as Michael: both mean "Who is like God?"

Significance: the author of the Book of Micah. He was a prophet of the southern Kingdom of Judah at a time just after the destruction of the northern Kingdom of Israel. He told the people that the suffering in the north had been a punishment from God and that Judah would suffer the same fate.

Popularity: top 500 →

Micaiah (mee-KAY-uh)

Origin: from the same root as Michael: both mean "Who is like God?"

Significance: a prophet in the northern Kingdom of Israel during the reign of Ahab. He alone of 400 prophets warned Ahab against a campaign to retake the city of Ramoth-gilead, foretelling a great defeat and Ahab's death in battle.

Popularity: uncommon ↑

Nathan

Origin: Hebrew meaning "give," implying the giving of a gift.

Significance: a prophet who revealed to David that one of his descendants would be the Messiah. He also prophesied that David's first child with Bathsheba would die because David plotted the death of Bathsheba's husband, Uriah.

Popularity: top 100 ↓

Related names:

Nate – uncommon ↓

Obed

Origin: Hebrew meaning "servant."

Significance: the son of Boaz and Ruth, and the grandfather of King David through his son, Jesse.

Popularity: endangered →

Oren

Origin: Hebrew meaning "pine tree."

Significance: mentioned in a genealogy of King David in 1 Chronicles.

Popularity: endangered →

Salem

Origin: Hebrew meaning "peace."

Significance: a city in Canaan. Separately, it is sometimes used as a name for Jerusalem, which David established as the capital of the united Kingdom of Israel.

Popularity: ♂♀ uncommon ↑

Samuel

Origin: Hebrew meaning "God has heard."

Significance: the last of the judges who led the tribes of Israel. He anointed Saul and David as the first kings of Israel.

Popularity: top 100 ↓

Related names:

Sam – short form – top 1000 ↓

Sammy – diminutive – uncommon ↓

Saul

Origin: Hebrew meaning "prayed (asked) for."

Significance: because the children of Israel asked for a king, Saul became the first king of the united Israelite tribes.

Popularity: top 500 ↓

Solomon

Origin: Hebrew meaning "peace."

Significance: the son of David. He was a famously wise leader who was the third and last king of the united Israelite tribes.

Popularity: top 500 ↑

Uriah

Origin: Hebrew meaning "Yahweh is my light."

Significance: the husband of Bathsheba, with whom David had an affair. He was a faithful soldier in David's army but was killed in battle through David's connivance.

Popularity: top 1000 ↑

Related names:

Urijah – top 1000 ↓

Zephaniah

Origin: Hebrew meaning "God is hidden."

Significance: a prophet during the reign of Josiah. He supported the King's efforts at reform and, like Jeremiah, chastised the people for their sins and foretold the destruction of Jerusalem.

Popularity: uncommon ↑

Zion

Origin: the Canaanite name of a hill near Jerusalem and also the name of a fortress on that hill.

Significance: Solomon built the First Temple on Mount Zion, and the name is often used to mean all of Jerusalem. By extension, Zion can also be a name for all of Israel and, by further extension, a name for the Jewish people.

Popularity: top 1000 →

The Israelites in Exile

Azariah

Origin: Hebrew meaning "helped by God."

Significance: With Mishael and Hananiah, he refused to bow down to a Babylonian idol and was sentenced to be burned. The three were, however, miraculously saved and did not die in the furnace.

Popularity: ♂♀ top 1000 ↑

Cyrus

Origin: a Persian name of uncertain meaning.

Significance: a great Persian emperor who conquered Babylon after Babylon had conquered Judah. He allowed the Israelites to the return to their homeland.

Popularity: top 500 ↑

Daniel

Origin: Hebrew meaning "God is my judge."

Significance: one of the Israelites who grew up in the Babylonian court. He was able to interpret the King's dreams, so he was raised to a position of great power within Babylonia. Later Daniel's own dreams were interpreted for him by the angel Gabriel.

Popularity: top 10 ↓

Related names:

Danny – diminutive – top 500 ↓

Dan – short form – uncommon ↓

Danilo – form used in several Romance and Slavic languages – uncommon →

Darius

Origin: Persian meaning "he holds (possesses)," from a longer name meaning "holds firm the good."

Significance: Darius was a great Persian emperor at the time that the last of the Israelites were returning to Judah.

Popularity: top 1000 ↓

Related names:

Darío – Spanish – top 1000 →

Ezekiel

Origin: Hebrew meaning "God strengthens."

Significance: the author of the Book of Ezekiel. He prophesied the destruction of Jerusalem and, after its destruction, was exiled to Babylonia. Ezekiel also prophesied the rebuilding of the temple and the return from exile.

Popularity: top 500 ↑

Spelling variations: *Ezequiel*

Ezra

Origin: Hebrew meaning "help."

Significance: Ezra led a group of exiles back to Jerusalem, where he also brought them back to right worship and observance of God's laws.

Popularity: top 500 ↑

Related names:

Esdras – Biblical Greek – endangered →

Gabriel

Origin: Hebrew meaning "God is my strength."

Significance: the name of the angel who appeared to Daniel to tell him the meaning of his visions.

Popularity: top 100 ↓

Related names:

Gabe – endangered ↓

Cross-reference: Gabriel is also listed in chapter 8, "Christian Concepts and Virtues" (page 123).

Jayden

Origin: variant spelling of Jadon, a Hebrew name, possibly meaning "He judges."

Significance: Jadon is mentioned in the Book of Nehemiah as one of the men who worked to rebuild the walls of Jerusalem after the exile of the Israelites had ended.

Popularity: top 100 ↓

Spelling variations: *Jaden, Jaiden, Jaydon, Jadon*

Joel

Origin: Hebrew meaning "Yahweh is God."

Significance: the author of the Book of Joel. He was a prophet who commanded the people to repent and foretold future blessings.

Popularity: top 500 ↓

Malachi

Origin: Hebrew meaning "my messenger."

Significance: the author of the Book of Malachi. After the Israelites returned to Judah and Jerusalem was being rebuilt, the prophet Malachi worked to prevent the people from once again worshipping foreign gods and taught them observe God's laws more closely.

Popularity: top 500 →

Spelling variations: *Malakai, Malaki*

Meshach

Origin: the Babylonian name for Misael. It may be related to the Babylonian moon god, Aku.

Significance: see Misael.

Popularity: endangered →

Michael

Origin: Hebrew meaning "Who is like God?"

Significance: an archangel who was revealed to Daniel as the protector of Israel and its people.

Popularity: top 10 ↓

Related names:

Miguel – Iberian – top 500 ↓

Mitchell – form of Michael brought back to Britain by Crusaders; originally used as a last name – top 1000 ↓

Mike – English short form – top 1000 ↓

Mikhail – Slavic – uncommon ↑

Mick – English short form – endangered →

Mickey – diminutive of Mick – endangered →

Miguelangel – Spanish – uncommon ↓

Michelangelo – Italian – endangered ↓

Spelling variations: *Micheal*

Cross-reference: Because the archangel Michael plays a prominent role in the Book of Revelation, the name is also listed the section on "Christian Concepts" in chapter 8 (page 124).

Misael

Origin: from the same root as Michael: both mean "Who is like God?"

Significance: With Azariah and Hananiah, Misael refused to bow down to a Babylonian idol and was sentenced to be burned. The three were, however, miraculously saved and did not die in the furnace.

Popularity: top 1000 →

Related names:

Mishael – endangered →

Obadiah

Origin: Hebrew meaning "servant of Yahweh."

Significance: there may be as many as a dozen Biblical figures named Obadiah. The most well-known was a prophet and the author of the Book of Obadiah. He hid the hundred prophets from the persecutions of Jezebel and spent his own fortune in feeding and caring for them.

Popularity: endangered ↑

Zachariah

Origin: variant spelling of Zechariah, Hebrew meaning "Yahweh remembers."

Significance: a prophet at the end of the Babylonian exile and the author of the Book of Zechariah. He encouraged the people by reminding them of their heritage and foretelling the blessings God would give them.

Popularity: top 500 →

Related names:

Zack – uncommon →

Spelling variations: *Zechariah*

Zeke

Origin: short form of Ezekiel, Hebrew meaning "God strengthens."

Significance: see Ezekiel.

Popularity: top 1000 ↑

Old Testament Traditions

Figures from the Book of Tobit are included in this section. Note that Tobit is part of the Catholic and Orthodox cannons; it is not, however, canonical to Protestants. Similarly, the role of Uriel is not part of the Protestant tradition.

Azariah

Origin: Hebrew meaning "helped by God."

Significance: in the Book of Tobit, the angel Raphael gave Azariah as his name while he was in human form.

Popularity: ♂♀ top 1000 ↑

Jebediah

Origin: a blend of Jeb and Jedediah. It is an American coinage that was first used in 1973.

Significance: Jeb has no special significance in Christianity. See Jedidiah (page 103).

Popularity: endangered →

Related names:

Jeb – the first three initials of James Ewell Brown Stuart, a Confederate general during the Civil War. It is most commonly used as a nickname for boys with the same initials, such as John Ellis Bush, of the presidential family – endangered →

Rafael

Origin: Hebrew meaning "God heals."

Significance: a central figure in the Book of Tobit, in which he helps Tobit, Tobias, and Sarah.

Popularity: top 500 ↓

Spelling variations: *Raphael*

Tobias

Origin: Hebrew meaning "God is good."

Significance: with the help of the angel Raphael, Tobias cured his father of blindness. He also drove away a demon that had plagued a woman named Sarah, whom he then married.

Popularity: top 500 ↑

Related names:

Toby – top 1000 ↑

Tobin – uncommon →

Uriel

Origin: Hebrew meaning "God is my light."

Significance: an archangel who was sent to help Ezra. Uriel answered Ezra's questions and explained the meanings of his visions.

Popularity: top 500 ↓

Yadiel (YAH-dee-el)

Origin: Hebrew, of unknown meaning.

Significance: in Jewish apocryphal texts, such as *The Sword of Moses* and the *Sefer Hechaloth*, Yadiel is an angel.

Popularity: uncommon ↓

Hebrew Names

Most Old Testament and many New Testament names are Hebrew in origin. There are, however, Hebrew names that do not appear in the Bible at all. Those non-Biblical Hebrew names that are in general use are included in this section.

Ari

Meaning: Hebrew meaning "lion."

Popularity: top 500 ↑

Ira

Meaning: Hebrew meaning "watchful."

Popularity: uncommon ↑

Jaron

Meaning: Hebrew meaning "to sing, shout, make joyful noise."

Popularity: uncommon ↓

Chapter 7: The New Testament

People and Places in the Life of Jesus

Andrés

Origin: Spanish form of the Greek name Andreas, meaning "manly."

Significance: see Andrew.

Popularity: top 500 ↓

Related names:

Anderson – a last name meaning "Anders' son" – top 500 ↑

Andre – used in several Romance languages – top 500 ↓

Anders – Scandinavian form of Andreas – top 1000 ↑

Deandre – son of Andre – top 1000 ↓

Ender – variation of Anders – uncommon ↑

Andreas – original Greek form, also used in several Germanic languages – uncommon ↓

Andrew

Origin: English form of the Greek name Andreas, meaning "manly."

Significance: one of the Twelve Apostles.

Popularity: top 100 ↓

Related names:

Drew – short form – top 500 ↓

Andy – diminutive – top 500 ↓

Apollo

Origin: the name of a Greek god.

Significance: Apollos was an early and influential missionary.

Popularity: top1000 ↑

Related names:

Apollos – endangered →

Augustus

Origin: Latin meaning "exalted." The first emperor of Rome took *augustus* as a title, and it was used by succeeding emperors.

Significance: Caesar Augustus ordered the census that brought Mary and Joseph to Bethlehem.

Popularity: top 1000 ↑

Related names:

August – English – top 500 ↑

Gus – diminutive – uncommon ↑

Augusto – Spanish – endangered →

Auguste – French – endangered →

Cross-reference: Augustine and Austin are listed on page 137.

Barnabas

Origin: Aramaic meaning "one of the representatives."

Significance: an apostle, missionary, and companion of Paul.

Popularity: endangered →

Related names:

Barnaby – medieval French form – endangered →

Bartholomew

Origin: Aramaic meaning "son of Tolmay."

Significance: one of the Twelve Apostles.

Popularity: endangered →

Cesar

Origin: variant spelling of Caesar, a family name of the famous Roman ruler Gaius Julius Caesar. Caesar was later used as a title of Roman emperors.

Significance: Caesar Augustus ordered the census that brought Mary and Joseph to Bethlehem.

Popularity: top 500 ↓

Cornelius

Origin: a prestigious Roman family name.

Significance: Cornelius and his household were the first Gentile converts (Acts 10).

Popularity: uncommon ↓

Cross-reference: Cornelius is also listed in chapter 10 (page 138).

Jace

Origin: short form of Jason.

Significance: see Jason.

Popularity: top 100 ↑

Spelling variations: *Jase, Jayce*

Jack

Origin: usually regarded as a form of the English name John; however, it is sometimes taken as the English form of French Jacques, a form of James.

Significance: see John and James.

Popularity: top 100 →

Jacobo

Origin: a Spanish form of James. It has the same origin as the name Jacob. Both are derived from Hebrew like this: Hebrew Ya'aqob > Greek Iakobos > Latin Jacobus.

Significance: see James.

Popularity: endangered →

Cross-reference: Hebrew Ya'aqob is also the origin of Jacob, which is listed in chapter 6 (page 96).

Jacques

Origin: French form of James, derived from Hebrew like this: Hebrew Ya'aqob > Greek Iakobos > Latin Jacobus > French Jacques.

Significance: see James.

Popularity: endangered ↓

Jairus (JYE-russ)

Origin: Hebrew meaning "He enlightens."

Significance: Jesus resurrected Jairus's daughter.

Popularity: endangered →

Cross-reference: Jairus is the New Testament form of Jair, which is listed in chapter 6 (page 100).

James

Origin: the New Testament form of Jacob, Hebrew meaning "supplanter." It is derived from Hebrew like this: Hebrew Ya'aqob > Greek Iakobos > Latin Jacobus > Late Latin Jacomus > French Gemmes > English James.

Significance: There were two apostles named James: James the brother of Jesus; and James the son of Zebedee and Salome, who was also the brother of the apostle John.

Popularity: top 10 ↓

Related names:

Jaime (HYE-mee) – Spanish – top 500 ↓

Jamie – diminutive – ♂♀ top 1000 ↓

Jimmy – diminutive – top 1000 ↓

Jessejames – English combination of Jesse and James – endangered →

Jameson

Origin: an English last name meaning "James's son."

Significance: see James.

Popularity: top 500 ↑

Related names:

Jamison – top 500 ↑

Jason

Origin: Greek meaning "healer."

Significance: an early disciple and missionary (Acts 17).

Popularity: top 100 ↓

Spelling variations: *Jayceon, Jayson*

Jordan

Origin: from the Jordan River, which has its source in Lebanon and flows into the Dead Sea. The name comes from Hebrew *yarden*, meaning "to descend."

Significance: Jesus was baptized by John the Baptist in the Jordan River.

Popularity: top 100 ↓

Related names:

Judson – a last name meaning "Jordan's son." It was brought back from the Holy Land by Crusaders. – top 1000 ↑

Jordany – endangered →

Spelling variations: *Jordyn, Jorden*

Joseph

Origin: Hebrew meaning "God will add," implying the addition of children to a family.

Significance: there are several Biblical figures named Joseph, including the man who married Mary, and one of their sons.

Popularity: top 100 ↓

Related names:

José – Iberian form – top 100 ↓

Joe – short form – top 1000 ↓

Joey – diminutive – top 1000 ↓

Giuseppe – Italian – uncommon →

Jody – diminutive – ♂♀ endangered ↓

Josemanuel – endangered →

Josecarlos – endangered →

Joseantonio – endangered →

Josemaria – endangered →

Josemiguel – endangered →

Joseangel – endangered →

Joseluis – endangered ↓

Joeangel – endangered →

Cross-reference: Joseph, son of Jacob and Rebecca, was an important figure in Genesis. See chapter 6, "The Old Testament" (page 96).

Jude

Origin: from Latin meaning "to praise."

Significance: a brother of Jesus. Also Judas Thaddeus was one of the Twelve Apostles and the author of the Epistle of Jude.

Popularity: top 500 ↑

Justus

Origin: Latin, signifying fair treatment of people, especially under the law.

Significance: Joseph Justus, also call Barsabbas, was a disciple of Jesus and was considered as a replacement for Judas Iscariot after his betrayal (Acts 1:23-26).

Popularity: top 1000 →

Related names:

Justo – endangered →

Lazarus

Origin: Latin form of Eleazar, Hebrew meaning "my God has helped."

Significance: Lazarus of Bethany was resurrected by Jesus four days after he (Lazarus) died.

Popularity: uncommon ↑

Related names:

Lazaro – used in several Romance languages – endangered ↓

Luca

Origin: short form of Lucas used in many Romance and Slavic languages.

Significance: see Luke.

Popularity: top 500 ↑

Spelling variations: *Luka, Lucca*

Lucas

Origin: Latin meaning "from Lucania," a place in Italy.

Significance: see Luke.

Popularity: top 100 ↑

Spelling variations: *Lukas*

Lucius

Origin: Latin meaning "light."

Significance: mentioned in Acts as an early missionary and Church leader in Syria.

Popularity: uncommon →

Luke

Origin: short form of Lucas, Latin meaning "from Lucania," a place in Italy.

Significance: a companion of the apostle Paul and one of the four authors of the Gospels.

Popularity: top 100 ↑

Marcelo

Origin: a variation of Marcellus in several Romance languages. Ultimately, it means "consecrated to Mars."

Significance: see Mark.

Popularity: top 1000 ↑

Related names:

Marcel – French short form of Marcellus – top 1000 →

Marlon – diminutive of Marcel – top 1000 ↓

Marcellus – Roman diminutive of Marcus – uncommon →

Marcus

Origin: an older, Latin form of Mark.

Significance: see Mark.

Popularity: top 500 ↓

Related names:

Marcos – top 500 ↓

Marco – top 500 ↓

Demarcus – uncommon ↓

Marcoantonio – endangered ↓

Spelling variations: *Markus*

Mark

Origin: short form of Marcus.

Significance: a companion of the apostle Peter and one of the four authors of the Gospels.

Popularity: top 500 ↓

Related names:

Marcanthony – endangered ↓

Spelling variations: *Marc*

Mateo

Origin: a Spanish and Italian form of Matthew.

Significance: see Matthew.

Popularity: top 500 ↑

Spelling variations: *Matteo*

Mathias

Origin: variant spelling of Matthais, used in Biblical Greek as the spelling for a second apostle named Matthew, chosen by Jesus after Judas's betrayal.

Significance: see Matthew.

Popularity: top 500 ↑

Related names:

Matias – top 1000 ↑

Spelling variations: *Matthias*

Matthew

Origin: Hebrew meaning "Gift of God."

Significance: one of the Twelve Apostles and one of the four authors of the Gospels.

Popularity: top 10 ↓

Related names:

Matt – endangered →

Spelling variations: *Mathew*

Nathaniel

Origin: Hebrew meaning "given of God."

Significance: a friend of the apostle Philip and a disciple of Jesus (John 1).

Popularity: top 100 ↓

Related names:

Nate – uncommon ↓

Spelling variations: *Nathaniel*

Nazareth

Origin: a town during the life of Jesus, Nazareth is now a large city in modern-day Israel.

Significance: the town where Jesus grew up.

Popularity: endangered →

Paul

Origin: Latin meaning "small."

Significance: Jesus appeared to Paul after the crucifixion. Paul preached the gospel to the Gentiles and helped to establish and strengthen new churches. He is also the author of fourteen epistles that form part of the New Testament.

Popularity: top 500 ↓

Related names:

Pablo – Spanish – top 500 ↓

Paulo – Portuguese – endangered →

Paolo – Italian – endangered ↓

Pavel – Slavic – endangered →

Peter

Origin: Greek meaning "stone."

Significance: one of the Twelve Apostles and an important leader of the early Church. He is regarded by Catholics as the first pope.

Popularity: top 500 ↓

Related names:

Pedro – Spanish – top 500 ↓

Pietro – Italian – endangered →

Pete – English short form – endangered ↓

Phillip

Origin: Greek meaning "horse-loving."

Significance: one of the Twelve Apostles.

Popularity: top 500 ↓

Spelling variations: *Philip*

Pierce

Origin: an English and Irish variation of Peter, from Pierres, an Old French form. It is Greek meaning "stone."

Significance: see Peter.

Popularity: top 500 ↑

Related names:

Pierson – a last name meaning "Pierce's son" – uncommon ↑

Pierre – French form of Peter – uncommon →

Seamus

Origin: Irish form of James.

Significance: see James.

Popularity: top 1000 →

Semaj

Origin: James spelled backward.

Significance: see James.

Popularity: top 1000 ↓

Silas

Origin: contraction of Silvanus, Latin meaning "of the woods."

Significance: a companion of Paul, with whom he traveled as a missionary.

Popularity: top 500 ↑

Spelling variations: *Sylas*

Simon

Origin: Hebrew meaning "He has heard."

Significance: another name of the apostle Peter and the name of one of Jesus's brothers.

Popularity: top 500 ↑

Cross-reference: Simon is also the name of one of Jacob's sons and is listed in "The Old Testament" (page 97).

Thaddeus

Origin: Greek form of Thaddai, an Aramaic name that may mean "heart."

Significance: Judas Thaddeus was one of the Twelve Apostles.

Popularity: top 1000 ↑

Related names:

Tadeo – Spanish – uncommon ↑

Tad – endangered →

Thad – endangered ↓

Thomas

Origin: Aramaic meaning "twin."

Significance: Thomas was one of the Twelve Apostles and the only one who doubted Jesus's resurrection.

Popularity: top 100 ↓

Related names:

Tommy – top 1000 ↓

Tom – endangered ↓

Spelling variations: *Tomas*

Cross-reference: Thomas is also the name of two important medieval saints and is included in the section titled "Saints of the Middle Ages" in chapter 10 (page 155).

Timothy

Origin: from Greek meaning "honoring God."

Significance: a young disciple and friend of the apostle Paul. Paul wrote Timothy two epistles that comprise two books of the Bible. Timothy also worked with Paul on several Biblical texts.

Popularity: top 500 ↓

Related names:

Tim – endangered →

Timmy – endangered ↓

Titus

Origin: Roman first name meaning "honorable." It comes from the legendary Sabine king Titus Tatianus.

Significance: a companion of the apostle Paul and an early Church leader.

Popularity: top 500 ↑

Related names:

Tito – used in several Romance languages – endangered →

Zachary

Origin: English form of Zachariah, Hebrew meaning "Yahweh remembers."

Significance: used in English translations of the Bible as the name of the father of John the Baptist.

Popularity: top 100 ↓

Related names:

Zack – uncommon →

Spelling variations: *Zackary*

John

Of all the names used in America, not one has more variations than John. It was one of the first Biblical names used in England, in the medieval French form Jehan. The name spread throughout the British Isles, where each country developed its own spelling, pronunciation, and nicknames, most of which came to America with early colonists or later immigrants. In addition to the many British variations, the US has versions of John from Italy, Spain, Germany, Poland, and Russia.

John was the name of two men who were very close to Jesus: his cousin, John the Baptist; and the apostle John, who is believed to have written five of the books in the New Testament. The Hebrew form of the name is Yohanan, meaning "He has favored." It was transliterated into New Testament Greek as Ioannes and became Iouavannes in Late Latin, the source of *v*-variations like Evan, Ivan, and Giovanni.

Evan

Origin: Welsh form of John.

Popularity: top 100 ↓

Related names:

Van – top 1000 →

Evans – endangered ↑

Giovanni

Origin: Italian form of John.

Popularity: top 500 →

Related names:

Gianni – top 1000 ↑

Jovanni – top 1000 →

Jionni – uncommon ↑

Gian – uncommon →

Gio – endangered ↑

Spelling variations: *Giovani, Giovanny*

Ian

Origin: Scottish form of John.

Popularity: top 100 →

Spelling variations: *Ean*

Ivan

Origin: Slavic form of John.

Popularity: top 500 →

Related names:

Van – short form – top 1000 ↑

Navi – Ivan spelled backward: it is a nickname for the constellation Cassiopeia, named for astronaut Gus Grissom, whose middle name was Ivan – ♀ endangered →

Jack

Origin: contraction of Jankin, a Germanic diminutive of Jan, which is a form of John.

Popularity: top 100 →

Related names:

Jax – nickname – top 500 ↑

Jake – medieval English – top 500 ↓

Jackie – ♂♀ endangered ↓

Cross-reference: Jack is also a form of James. For more information, see the previous section of this chapter, "People and Places in the Life of Jesus" (page 111).

Jackson

Origin: an English last name meaning "Jack's son."

Popularity: top 100 ↑

Spelling variations: *Jaxon, Jaxson, Jaxen*

Jaxton

Origin: an English last name meaning "Jack's town."

Popularity: top 500 ↑

Jean

Origin: modern French form, from Latin Jouannes. In Latin writing, *i* and *j* are somewhat interchangeable, and they are said the same way. However, *j* has different sounds in various European languages. This is one cause of the many John-variations.

Popularity: uncommon ↓

Jensen

Origin: a Scandinavian last name meaning "Jens' son."

Popularity: top 500 ↑

Related names:

Jens – a Germanic form of John – endangered →

Jennings – equivalent to "little John"; used for the younger of two Jens, as when a father and son both bear the name – endangered →

Joán (jo-AHN)

Origin: Catalan form of Juan/John.

Popularity: Joan (JOWN) is a traditional English girls' name, but the Catalan boys' name Joán is now more common in the US. – ♂♀ endangered →

Johan (YO-hahn)

Origin: short form of Johannes.

Popularity: top 1000 →

Related names:

Hans – contracted short form of Johannes – uncommon →

Johannes (yo-HAHN-ess) – Germanic form of John – endangered →

Hanson – a last name meaning "Hans' son" – endangered →

Jan (YAHN) – contraction of Johan – endangered ↓

John

Origin: English form of French Jean.

Popularity: top 100 ↓

Related names:

Johnny – top 500 ↓

Jovan

Origin: a form of John in some Slavic languages.

Popularity: uncommon ↓

Juan (WAHN)

Origin: Spanish form of John.

Popularity: top 100 ↓

Related names:

Juanito – diminutive – endangered →

Sean

Origin: Irish form of John.

Popularity: top 500 ↓

Related names:

Shane – an English form of Sean – top 500 ↓

Spelling variations: *Shawn, Shaun*

Combination John Names

Giancarlo

Origin: combination of the Italian names Gian and Carlo. Carlo is a Germanic name, made famous by Charlemagne, the first Holy Roman emperor (page 144).

Popularity: top 100 →

Related names:

Giancarlos – endangered →

Juancarlos – endangered →

Johncarlos – endangered ↓

Gianfranco

Origin: combination of the Italian names Gian and Franco. Franco is a contracted form of Francesco, a nickname for Saint Francis of Assisi (page 146).

Popularity: endangered →

Gianluca

Origin: combination of the Italian names Gian and Luca. Luca is an Italian form of Luke, a companion of the apostle Paul and one of the four authors of the Gospels.

Popularity: uncommon ↑

Related names:

Johnluke – endangered ↑

Gianmarco

Origin: combination of the Italian names Gian and Marco. Marco is an Italian form of Mark, who was a companion of the apostle Peter and one of the four authors of the Gospels.

Popularity: endangered →

Johndavid

Origin: combination of the English names John and David. David was the second king of the united Israelite tribes.

Popularity: endangered →

Johnhenry

Origin: combination of the English names John and Henry. There were three medieval saints named Henry.

Popularity: endangered →

Johnmichael

Origin: combination of the English names John and Michael. Michael is an archangel whose defeat of Satan is described in the Book of Revelation.

Popularity: endangered ↓

Johnpaul

Origin: combination of the English names John and Paul. Paul preached the gospel to the Gentiles and helped to establish and strengthen new churches.

Popularity: uncommon →

Related names:

Juanpablo – endangered →

Juandiego

Origin: combination of the Spanish names Juan and Diego. Diego comes from a re-analysis of Sant Iago (Saint James) as San Diego.

Popularity: endangered →

Juanjose

Origin: combination of the Spanish names Juan and Jose. Jose is a Spanish form of Joseph, Mary's husband.

Popularity: endangered →

New Testament Traditions

This section includes names that have a strong association with the Catholic and Orthodox Churches but are not part of Protestant traditions.

Baltazar

Origin: Akkadian meaning "Ba'al protect the king."

Significance: one of the three Magi.

Popularity: endangered ↓

Carmelo

Origin: Hebrew meaning "fruitful field."

Significance: a reference to Mount Carmel. See "The Story of Stella Maris" (page 32).

Popularity: top 1000 →

Related names:

Carmen – Spanish – ♀ uncommon ↓

Carmine – Italian – endangered ↑

Diego

Origin: from a re-analysis of Sant Iago as San Diego. See Santiago for a complete etymology.

Significance: see James (page 111).

Popularity: top 500 ↓

Guadalupe

Origin: Guadalupe is a province in Mexico.

Significance: the Virgin Mary is said to have appeared to a peasant in 16th century Guadalupe.

Popularity: ♀ endangered ↓

Jasper

Origin: Persian meaning "treasurer."

Significance: one of the three Magi.

Popularity: top 500 ↑

Joaquin

Origin: Spanish form of Joachim, Hebrew meaning "lifted by Yahweh."

Significance: Joachim was Mary's father, and so the grandfather of Jesus.

Popularity: top 500 →

Santana

Origin: Spanish contraction of Santa Ana (Saint Anne).

Significance: Saint Anne was Mary's mother, and the grandmother of Jesus.

Popularity: top 1000 →

Santiago

Origin: used in Spanish and Portuguese, Santiago is a combined form of "Sant Iago," meaning "Saint James." Iago is derived from Hebrew: Hebrew Ya'aqob > Greek Iakobos > Spanish Iago.

Significance: see James (page 111).

Popularity: top 500 ↑

Related names:

Thiago – short form – top 500 ↑

Uriel

Origin: Hebrew meaning "God is my light."

Significance: When King Herod decreed that all boys under the age of two be killed, the archangel Uriel saved Elizabeth and her baby, John (the Baptist).

Popularity: top 500 →

Chapter 8: Christian Concepts and Virtues

Christian Concepts

In the summer of 2013, the parents of a baby in Tennessee brought forward a court case to settle a dispute over their child's last name. In addition to ruling on the last name, the judge ordered the child's first name, Messiah, to be changed to Martin. The judge's point was that the name Messiah could only be given to Jesus Christ and no other.

Many Americans disagreed with both the judge and the parents. Most people feel that it's not appropriate for a judge to tell parents what they can and cannot name their children. At the same time, many Christians were horrified by the name (which is actually quite popular at the moment). It seemed to show both excessive pride and an utter lack of respect for Jesus, though I suspect this was the opposite of the parents' intent. So, I want to say a word of caution about names like Messiah, Christos, and Savior. Perhaps a true Christian, however well-intentioned, should think twice before giving a child a name that many other Christians will feel is insulting to Jesus.

Abbott

Origin: Aramaic meaning "father." It is a traditional English last name.

Significance: an abbot is the head of a monastery.

Popularity: endangered ↑

Amen

Origin: Hebrew meaning "truth" or "so be it."

Significance: the word said at the end of a prayer.

Popularity: ♂♀ endangered ↑

Angel

Origin: Greek meaning "messenger."

Significance: angels are heavenly beings whom God sends to bear messages or to help people.

Popularity: top 100 ↓

Related names:

Angelo – top 500 ↓

Deangelo – top 1000 →

Arcangel – endangered ↑

Angelus – endangered →

Angelito – endangered →

Miguelangel – uncommon →

Michelangelo – endangered →

Joseangel – endangered →

Joeangel – endangered →

Luisangel – endangered ↓

Bishop

Origin: Greek meaning "overseer." It is a traditional English last name.

Significance: bishop was originally used for the leader of a Christian community. Now it refers to a clergyman, of some churches, who supervises a large group or area.

Popularity: uncommon →

Bless

Origin: an Old English word used by pagans to describe the consecration of an altar or offering.

Significance: to ask God to favor a person, place, or thing.

Popularity: endangered →

Cairo

Origin: Arabic meaning "the strong." It is the capital of Egypt.

Significance: coincidentally, the city name sounds exactly like *Chi Rho*, an early and popular Christian symbol. The *Chi Rho* comprises the first two letters of the Greek word *kristos*.

Popularity: uncommon ↑

Cannon

Origin: an English last name, Cannon comes from Greek meaning "rule."

Significance: an honorary title given to a senior clergyman or a church member who has been especially involved in church matters.

Popularity: top 1000 ↑

Christian

Origin: *Kristos* is a Greek translation of the Hebrew word *messiah*: both mean "anointed." See the entry for Messiah for more information.

Significance: the usual English word for a follower of Jesus.

Popularity: top 100 ↓

Related names:

Chris – short form – top 1000 ↓

Christiano – Spanish – endangered ↑

Spelling variations: *Cristian*

Christopher

Origin: Greek meaning "Christ-bearer." *Kristos* is a Greek translation of the Hebrew word *messiah*: both mean "anointed." See the entry for Messiah for more information.

Significance: Christopher was used by early Christians to mean they carried Jesus with them in their hearts.

Popularity: top 100 ↓

Related names:

Chris – short form – top 1000 ↓

Christobal – Spanish – endangered →

Spelling variations: *Kristopher, Cristopher*

Cross-reference: Christopher is also listed in chapter 9 (page 130).

Christos

Origin: *Kristos* is a Greek translation of the Hebrew word *messiah*: both mean "anointed."

Significance: a title for Jesus.

Popularity: endangered →

Crosby

Origin: Old Norse meaning "cross settlement."

Significance: traditionally a last name, Crosby probably referred to someone who lived near a stone cross erected as a road marker or a memorial to the dead.

Popularity: top 1000 ↑

Cruz

Origin: Spanish meaning cross.

Significance: a reference to the crucifixion.

Popularity: top 500 ↑

Related names:

Cruzito – Spanish diminutive – endangered →

Croix – French – endangered ↑

Cross – English – endangered →

Deacon

Origin: an English last name, Deacon comes from Greek meaning "servant."

Significance: a church office with specific duties and authority. Depending on time and place, a deacon can be a clergyman or a layman.

Popularity: top 500 ↑

Dean

Origin: from Latin meaning "leader of ten."

Significance: a clergyman who supervises a small group or area.

Popularity: top 500 ↑

Desiderio

Origin: Spanish form of the Latin name Desiderius, Latin meaning "desired, longed for."

Significance: early Christians used the name Desiderius to indicate a longing for Jesus.

Popularity: endangered →

Related names:

Desi – short form – ♂♀ endangered →

Didier – French – endangered →

Emmanuel

Origin: Hebrew meaning "God is with us."

Significance: Emmanuel is the name of the Messiah, prophesized in the Book of Isaiah and specified as Mary's child in the Gospel of Matthew.

Popularity: top 500 →

Spelling variations: *Emanuel, Immanuel*

Enzo

Origin: short form of Italian names ending with –*enzo*, such as Vincenzo and Lorenzo.

Significance: see Vincent in this section (page 126) and see Lorenzo in chapter 9, "Early Martyrs" (page133).

Popularity: top 500 ↑

Gabriel

Origin: Hebrew meaning "God is my strength."

Significance: the angel who appeared to tell Mary she would conceive Jesus. He also appeared to Zachariah to foretell the birth of his son, John the Baptist.

Popularity: top 100 ↓

Related names:

Gabe – endangered ↓

Cross-reference: Because Gabriel also appears to the prophet Daniel, this name is included in chapter 6, "The Old Testament" (page 106).

Godric

Origin: Old English meaning "power of God."

Significance: an Anglo-Saxon name that went out of use shortly after the Norman Conquest of England in 1066. It was revived in the US in 2009. Similar names which are no longer used include: Godfred/Godfrey, meaning "peace of God"; and Godwin, meaning "friend of God."

Popularity: endangered →

Haven

Origin: Old Norse meaning "harbor, port."

Significance: a place of safety.

Popularity: ♀ uncommon →

Iker

Origin: Basque meaning "visitation."

Significance: a reference to an event in the Gospel of Luke when Mary, pregnant with Jesus, visited her cousin Elizabeth, who was pregnant with John the Baptist.

Popularity: top 500 ↑

JC

Origin: the initials of Jesus Christ.

Significance: see Jesus.

Popularity: top 1000 →

Jesus (HAY-sus)

Origin: Hebrew meaning "Yahweh saves." It comes from the same root as the name Joshua.

Significance: Jesus was the manifestation of God on earth, in human form.

Popularity: Popular with Spanish-speakers, it is never given by English-speakers, who view it as too holy for general use – top 500 ↓

Kirk

Origin: Old Norse meaning "church." Originally, it was a last name for someone who lived near a church.

Significance: a church is a public place for Christian worship.

Popularity: uncommon ↓

Kyrie (KEER-ee-aay)

Origin: from *Kyrie eleison*, a pre-Christian, Greek prayer. The title means, "Lord have mercy."

Significance: Christians traditionally said the prayer during the lighting of lamps for Vespers.

Popularity: top 1000 ↑

Spelling variations: *Kyree*

Manuel

Origin: short form of Emmanuel, Hebrew meaning "God is with us."

Significance: see Emmanuel.

Popularity: top 500 ↓

Related names:

Manny – endangered →

Messiah

Origin: Hebrew meaning "anointed." It refers to one who would be the savior of his people.

Significance: Christians regard Jesus as the Messiah, prophesized in the Book of Isaiah and specified as Mary's child in the Gospel of Matthew.

Popularity: top 500 ↑

Michael

Origin: Hebrew meaning "Who is like God?"

Significance: an archangel whose defeat of Satan is described in the Book of Revelation.

Popularity: top 10 ↓

Related names:

Miguel – Iberian form of Michael – top 500 ↓

Mitchell – form of Michael brought back to Britain by Crusaders;

originally used as a last name – top 1000 ↓

Mike – English short form of Michael – top 1000 ↓

Mikhail – Slavic form of Michael – uncommon ↑

Mick – English short form of Michael – endangered →

Mickey – diminutive of Mick – endangered →

Miguelangel – uncommon →

Michelangelo – endangered →

Spelling variations: *Micheal*

Cross-reference: Michael is also listed in chapter 7 (page 107).

Noel

Origin: French variation of Latin *natalis dies*, meaning "birthday."

Significance: Noel is a reference to Christmas, the day Jesus was born.

Popularity: top 500 ↑

Palmer

Origin: an English last name, given to a person who had a palm branch.

Significance: in medieval England, it was usual to bring back a palm branch as evidence of a pilgrimage to the Holy Land.

Popularity: ♂♀ uncommon ↑

Pascal

Origin: from Latin *paschalis*, meaning "Easter." *Paschalis* is taken from Hebrew *Pesach*, meaning "Passover," because the two holidays fall close to one another in date.

Significance: traditionally a name for children born at Easter-time.

Popularity: spelled *Pascale* when used for girls – ♂♀ endangered →

René

Origin: French meaning "re-born."

Significance: given in honor of the resurrection of Jesus.

Popularity: spelled *Renée* when used for girls. ♂♀ top 1000 ↓

Related names:

Renato – Italian – endangered →

Romeo

Origin: Latin meaning "pilgrim to Rome."

Significance: it was common in the Middle Ages for people of means to travel to Rome to see holy places, such as the Vatican and the tombs of the apostles Peter and Paul.

Popularity: top 500 ↑

Salvador

Origin: "savior" in several Romance languages.

Significance: Salvador is a reference to Jesus as the Messiah.

Popularity: top 1000 ↓

Related names:

Salvatore – southern Italian – top 1000 →

Savior – English – endangered →

Shepherd

Origin: an English last name, given to someone who watches over sheep.

Significance: a common metaphor for Jesus and for Christian clergymen who are leaders of congregations.

Popularity: uncommon ↑

Victor

Origin: Latin meaning "conqueror."

Significance: early Christians used the name Victor as a reference to Jesus's victory over death.

Popularity: top 500 ↓

Vincent

Origin: short form of Vincentius, a Latin name meaning "conquering."

Significance: early Christians used Vincentius to honor Jesus's victory over death.

Popularity: top 500 →

Related names:

Vincenzo – Italian – top 1000 →

Vicente – Iberian – top 1000 ↓

Vince – short form – uncommon →

Vincente – Italian and Spanish – endangered ↓

Vinny – English diminutive – endangered →

Vinson – a last name meaning "Vin's son" – endangered →

Virtues

A serious mini-trend has popularized often off-beat virtue names for boys. Many of the names listed here have been used in the US for more than 100 years: Justice, Noble, Ace, and Sterling for example. Others are newer additions to the American Puritan tradition. While looking through the names in this section, keep in mind that there were boys on the *Mayflower* named Truelove, Wrestling, and Resolved.

Ace

Significance: someone who excels in some activity, especially sports. It's also the highest playing card.

Popularity: top 500 ↑

Alpha

Significance: the first letter of the Greek alphabet (Omega is the last). Used by early Christians because God is the Alpha and the Omega, the beginning and the end.

Popularity: endangered →

Arrow

Significance: someone who aims directly for his goals. It also recalls the expression "a straight arrow," used for someone who is unusually responsible and tries to do what's right.

Popularity: endangered ↑

Champ

Significance: short form of Champion. The short form implies the winner of a sporting event. The longer form conjures the image of someone who stands up for what is right and who defends the weak.

Popularity: endangered →

Related names:

Champion – endangered ↑

Ernest

Significance: Germanic—originally it meant "severe," but now it has the connotation of "sincere."

Popularity: top 1000 ↓

Related names:

Ernesto – used in several Romance languages – top 1000 ↓

Ernie – diminutive – endangered ↓

Frank

Significance: originally referred to the Franks, the powerful Germanic people who conquered the Celts in what is now France. As members of the ruling class, the Franks were able to speak freely, giving rise to the current meaning "direct and honest."

Popularity: top 500 ↓

Related names:

Frankie – top 1000 →

Cross-reference: Frank is also used as a short form of Frances. See the section titled, "Saints of the Middle Ages" in chapter 10 for more information (page 146).

Honor

Significance: in an internal sense, being honorable is having great moral integrity. The usual Biblical sense is more external: it is giving respect and obedience, as to God, parents, and laws.

Popularity: ♀ endangered ↑

Justice

Significance: the fair treatment of people, especially under the law.

Popularity: top 1000 →

Related names:

Justo – Spanish form of Justus – endangered →

Spelling variations: *Justus*

Cross-reference: Joseph Justus was a disciple of Jesus. See chapter 7, "The New Testament" for more information (page 112).

Justin

Significance: short form of Justinian, a Latin name derived from the word for justice.

Popularity: top 100 ↓

Related names:

Justino – endangered →

Knight

Significance: a mounted medieval warrior who swore to follow a code of behavior that exemplified fairness, courtesy, and honor.

Popularity: endangered ↑

Knowledge

Significance: truths and facts accumulated over time.

Popularity: endangered ↑

Legacy

Significance: in modern English, a legacy is that which is inherited by the family of one who has died. Legacy also refers to the sum effect of the actions taken during one's life.

Popularity: endangered ↑

Loyal

Significance: unyieldingly faithful.

Popularity: endangered ↑

Related names:

Loyalty – endangered ↑

Noble

Significance: having an exceptionally good character and high ideals.

Popularity: uncommon ↑

Pax

Significance: Latin meaning "peace."

Popularity: endangered ↑

Related names:

Pace – English meaning "peace." It was a medieval English last name. – endangered ↑

Sage

Significance: French meaning "wise."

Popularity: ♀ top 1000 →

Sincere

Significance: honestly expressing thoughts and feelings.

Popularity: top 1000 →

Steele

Significance: a metal alloy that is strong and hard to break.

Popularity: endangered ↑

Sterling

Significance: that which is sterling has a reputation and record that can withstand testing. Originally it referred to a type of coin used in medieval England. Now the pound sterling is the basic unit of British money. Sterling is also a term for silver that is 92% pure.

Popularity: top 1000 ↑

Truman

Significance: originally an English last name, probably given to someone who was especially honest and trustworthy.

Popularity: top 1000 ↑

Related names:

Truett – endangered ↑

Tru – ♂♀ endangered ↑

Truth – ♂♀ endangered →

Valor

Significance: bold courage; heroic bravery.

Popularity: endangered ↑

Chapter 9:
Early Martyrs

Aaron

Origin: possibly an ancient Egyptian name, but its meaning is not known.

Significance: martyred in Wales with a man named Julius c. 303.

Popularity: top 100 →

Spelling variations: *Aron*

Cross-reference: Aaron is more familiar as a Biblical name. See the section titled "Exodus and Early Years in Canaan" in chapter 6, "The Old Testament" for more information (page 98).

Adrian

Origin: a variation of Hadrian, the great Roman emperor from the town of Hadria, Italy.

Significance: an imperial guard of the Roman emperor Maximian. Adrian converted while participating in the torture of Christians and was himself imprisoned and later martyred.

Popularity: top 100 →

Related names:

Adriano – form of Adrian used in several Romance languages – endangered →

Alexander

Origin: Greek meaning "defender of men."

Significance: there have been several saints named Alexander, including four early martyrs and two early bishops.

Popularity: top 10 ↓

Related names:

Alex – short form – top 500 ↓

Alec – Gaelic short form – top 500 ↓

Alejandro – Spanish – top 500 ↓

Alessandro – Italian – top 1000 →

Alexandro – used in several Romance languages – uncommon ↓

Lex – short form – endangered →

Alistair – Gaelic form – uncommon ↑

Sasha – Slavic diminutive. It is traditionally more common for boys than girls, but in the US it is used almost exclusively for girls. – ♀ endangered →

Spelling variations: *Alexzander*

Blaise

Origin: Latin meaning "lisping."

Significance: Saint Blaise's reputation as a healer brought sick people to him from far and wide. His miraculous cures, virtuous behavior, and praise of Christianity won him many followers. He was martyred in 316.

Popularity: top 1000 ↑

Cassian

Origin: from Cassia, the name of an ancient Roman family.

Significance: there were two martyrs named Cassian: 1) At the trial of a Christian centurion named Marcellus, who was sentenced to death, Cassian of Tangier, a court recorder, declared his faith and was subsequently martyred. 2) Cassian of Imola was a school headmaster in Italy, martyred by his own students under a general persecution.

Popularity: endangered →

Christopher

Origin: Greek meaning "Christ-bearer." *Kristos* comes from a Greek translation of the Hebrew word *messiah*—both mean "anointed."

Significance: a Christian martyred in 251. There are many legends about Saint Christopher, but little is certain about his life or death.

Popularity: top 100 ↓

Related names:

Chris – short form – top 1000 ↓

Christobal – Spanish – endangered →

Spelling variations: *Kristopher, Cristopher*

Cross-reference: Christopher is also listed in the section on "Christian Concepts" in chapter 8 (page 122).

Damian

Origin: Greek meaning "to tame."

Significance: twins Damian and Cosmas were physicians who treated the sick for free. With their three younger brothers, they were martyred in 287.

Popularity: top 500 ↑

Spelling variations: *Damien, Damion*

Demetrius

Origin: Greek meaning "follower of Demeter."

Significance: a Greek Christian from a prestigious family, martyred in 270.

Popularity: top 1000 ↓

Related names:

Dimitri – top 1000 →

Dennis

Origin: Greek, from the name of the god Dionysus.

Significance: martyred around the year 250. He was the bishop of Paris at the time and is a patron saint of that city.

Popularity: top 500 ↓

Related names:

Denny – endangered ↓

Donato

Origin: Italian form of Donatus, Latin meaning "given."

Significance: 4th century bishop who was martyred under Julian the Apostate. Julian was a Roman emperor who outlawed Christianity after Constantine I had declared it legal.

Popularity: endangered →

Related names:

Donatello – endangered ↑

Enzo

Origin: short form of Italian names ending with *–enzo*, such as Lorenzo and Vincenzo.

Significance: see Lorenzo in this section (page 133) and Vincenzo in the section on "Christian Concepts" in chapter 8 (page 126).

Popularity: top 500 ↑

Esteban

Origin: Spanish form of the Greek name Stefanos, meaning "wreath, crown," implying an honor that has been won and rewarded.

Significance: see Steven.

Popularity: top 500 →

Eugene

Origin: Greek meaning "well-born."

Significance: there have been three saints named Eugene, the earliest of whom was the first bishop of Paris, martyred in 275.

Popularity: top 1000 ↓

Related names:

Eugenio – endangered →

Gene – endangered ↓

Fabian

Origin: from Fabia, a patrician Roman family name.

Significance: as pope, Fabian was a conciliatory figure who generally maintained good relations with the Roman government. However, he was martyred during a widespread persecution of Christians in 250.

Popularity: top 500 →

Felix

Origin: Latin meaning "lucky."

Significance: the name of at least five early martyrs, the first of whom died under the emperor Nero in 68. The name was also borne by numerous other saints as well as five popes.

Popularity: top 500 ↑

Genaro

Origin: Spanish form of Januarius, a Roman family name meaning "archway." It is also the Latin word for January.

Significance: born into a pagan family, Januarius converted when he was 15 years old and later became the bishop of Naples. He was martyred in 305 under the emperor Diocletian.

Popularity: endangered ↓

George

Origin: Greek meaning "farmer."

Significance: born into a Christian family, George served as a soldier in the Roman army. He was martyred as part of an edict to purge the army of Christian soldiers, and as he was tortured in the arena, more than 600 people either revealed their faith or converted on the spot, and were subsequently martyred themselves. This included the empress, Alexandra, who revealed her faith by entering the arena and bowing down to George, upon which both were immediately killed on orders of the emperor, Diocletian.

Popularity: top 500 →

Related names:

Jordy – Dutch diminutive – top 1000 →

Gino – Italian diminutive of several names, including Giorgio – top 1000 →

Giorgio – Italian – endangered ↑

Gio – short form of Giorgio and Giovanni (page 117) – endangered ↑

Ignacio

Origin: Spanish form of Ignatius, from the Roman family name Egnacia.

Significance: Saint Ignatius of Antioch was an early church leader and disciple of the apostle John. He was martyred c. 107, having been thrown to wild animals in the Colosseum of Rome.

Popularity: uncommon ↓

Related names:

Ignatius – English – endangered ↑

Cross-reference: Ignacio is also listed in chapter 10 (page 149).

Jarvis

Origin: English form of Gervais, possibly a Germanic name. The first element of the name may be *gar* meaning "spear"; the meaning of the second element is not known.

Significance: in the 2nd century, Gervasius and Protasius were twin brothers living in Milan. They were martyred together after both of their parents had already been martyred.

Popularity: uncommon →

Jorge (HORE-heh)

Origin: Spanish form of George, Greek meaning "farmer."

Significance: see George.

Popularity: top 500 ↓

Julian

Origin: from Julia, an ancient Roman family name.

Significance: there were two martyrs named Julian: both died under the emperor Diocletian in Antioch, a Greek city (now in Turkey).

Popularity: top 100 ↑

Related names:

Juliano – Portuguese – endangered →

Spelling variations: *Julien*

Cross-reference: Julian is also listed in chapter 10 (page 139).

Julius

Origin: Roman masculine of Julia, an ancient Roman family name.

Significance: there were two martyrs named Julius, both of whom died under Diocletian: 1) One was a soldier who had served 27 years in the Roman army. 2) The other was martyred in Wales with man named Aaron (page 129).

Popularity: top 500 →

Related names:

Julio – Spanish – top 500 ↓

Kai

Origin: short form of Caius, an Etruscan name possibly meaning "rejoice." In ancient times, Caius and Gaius were both pronounced GAI-us. This was because *c* was used to represent both the *k* and *g* sounds until the 3rd century BC.

Significance: Gaius was pope from 283-296 and is thought to have been martyred under Diocletian.

Popularity: top 500 ↑

Related names:

Caius – uncommon ↑

Gaius – endangered ↑

Lawrence

Origin: Latin meaning "from Laurentium," an ancient Roman city.

Significance: an early church deacon martyred in 258 under a general persecution of church officials.

Popularity: top 500 ↓

Related names:

Larry – English – top 1000 ↓

Lawson – Lar's son – top 500 ↑

Lars – Germanic short form – endangered →

Laurent – French – endangered →

Law – English short form – endangered →

Lawton – Law's town – endangered →

Loren – English short form – endangered ↓

Leonidas

Origin: Greek meaning "son of a lion."

Significance: there were several martyrs named Leonidas, the earliest of whom was martyred in Alexandria, Egypt in 202.

Popularity: top 1000 ↑

Related names:

Leo – top 100 ↑

Leon – top 500 ↑

Leonel – top 500 →

Cross-reference: Leo is also the name of thirteen popes and is listed, with Leon and Leonel, in the section titled "The Church to 500 AD" in chapter 10 (page 139).

Lorenzo

Origin: in several Romance languages, Lorenzo is a form of Lawrence, Latin meaning "from Laurentium," an ancient Roman city.

Significance: see Lawrence.

Popularity: top 500 ↑

Related names:

Renzo – endangered →

Lucian

Origin: variation of Lucius, Latin meaning "light."

Significance: there were two martyrs named Lucian: 1) a Roman missionary martyred in 290 in Beauvais, France, where a diocese was founded in his honor; 2) a scholar and ascetic martyred in 312 in Antioch, a Greek city (now in Turkey).

Popularity: top 1000 →

Mack

Origin: Scottish short form of Makr, a Scandinavian form of Magnus. The name entered Scotland via the Shetlands, a group of islands off the northeast coast of Scotland that was controlled by Scandinavian peoples for much of the Middle Ages.

Significance: see Magnus.

Popularity: top 1000 ↑

Magnus

Origin: a Latin name meaning "great." It was famously used in Scandinavia as a royal name styled after Charlemagne's Latin name, Carolus Magnus.

Significance: there have been several saints named Magnus: the earliest was a 2nd century Italian bishop and missionary martyred during widespread persecutions.

Popularity: top 1000 ↑

Maurice

Origin: French form of Maurus, a Latin name meaning "person from Mauritania" (now Morocco and northern Algeria).

Significance: a Roman soldier and leader of a legion composed entirely of Christians. He and all of the 6,600 men of his legion were martyred in 287 for refusing the emperor's command to kill local Christians.

Popularity: top 1000 ↓

Related names:

Mauricio – Spanish – top 1000 ↓

Morris – English – uncommon →

Morrison – English last name meaning "Morris's son" – endangered ↑

Maximilian

Origin: short form of Maximilianus, a Latin diminutive of Maximus, meaning "greatest."

Significance: martyred in 295 for refusing to join the Roman army. He felt that the service would conflict with his obligations as a Christian.

Popularity: top 500 →

Related names:

Max – short form – top 500 →

Maximiliano – Iberian – top 500 ↑

Massimiliano – Italian – endangered →

Nestor

Origin: a figure from Greek mythology: He was one of the Argonauts and an adviser to the Greeks during the Trojan War.

Significance: there were two martyrs names Nestor: 1) Nestor of Magydos was an early bishop martyred in 250 because of his great influence in the Christian community. 2) At the turn of the 4th century, Nestor of Thessaloniki entered the Roman arena of his own accord to fight a notoriously vicious gladiator, whom he killed. He was then martyred on the emperor's orders.

Popularity: uncommon ↓

Quentin

Origin: variation of Quintus, Latin meaning "fifth." The name was originally used for the 5th child, the 5th son, or for a child born in the 5th month.

Significance: a Roman missionary from a prestigious family. He was martyred in 287 in a place that is now in northern France, named Saint-Quentin after him.

Popularity: top 500 →

Related names:

Quincy – top 1000 →

Spelling variations: *Quinton, Quintin*

Rufus

Origin: Latin meaning "red," implying red hair.

Significance: there were at least 10 early martyrs named Rufus.

Popularity: endangered →

Sebastian

Origin: meaning "from Sebaste," the name of many Greek towns. *Sebaste* is the Greek translation of *august*, Latin meaning "exalted." It was given to towns in honor of Ceasar Augustus as well as later Roman emperors who bore the title "augustus."

Significance: a captain of the guards of the emperor Diocletian. Sebastian performed miracles and converted many people. He was martyred in 288 on the orders of the emperor.

Popularity: top 100 ↑

Related names:

Bastian – uncommon ↑

Sebastiano – endangered →

Sidney

Origin: a contracted form of Saint Denis.

Significance: see Dennis.

Popularity: traditionally a boys' name, but now more common for girls. The spelling *Sidney* is slightly more popular for girls than boys while *Sydney* is used almost exclusively for girls. – ♂♀ uncommon ↓

Related names:

Sid – endangered →

Steven (STEE-vuhn)

Origin: from the Greek name Stefanos, meaning "wreath, crown," implying an honor that has been won and rewarded. In the US, it is usually pronounced with a *v* as the middle sound, though some people prefer the older *f* pronunciation.

Significance: a teacher and active member of the early Church. Stephen was a Jewish convert and is believed to be the first Christian martyr, killed by Jewish authorities for blasphemy.

Popularity: top 500 ↓

Related names:

Stefan – alternate spelling indicating the *f* pronunciation – top 1000 →

Steve – short form – top 1000 ↓

Stefano – Italian – endangered →

Etienne – French – endangered →

Spelling variations: *Stephen*

Terrance

Origin: from the Roman family name Terentia.

Significance: after witnessing the crucifixion of the apostle Peter, Terrance is said to have converted and then to have been martyred himself.

Popularity: top 1000 ↓

Related names:

Terry – top 1000 ↓

Spelling variations: *Terrence*

Theodore

Origin: Greek meaning "gift of God."

Significance: there are many saints named Theodore: the first was a martyr persecuted under Hadrian.

Popularity: top 500 ↑

Related names:

Theo (THEE-o) – top 1000 ↑

Ted – endangered →

Teddy – endangered →

Teodoro – used in several Romance languages – endangered ↓

Teo (TAY-o) – short form of Teodoro – endangered →

Dietrich – German short form of Theodoric – endangered ↑

Fyodor – Russian – endangered →

Valentino

Origin: Latin meaning "strong."

Significance: there are three saints named Valentine, all martyred at different times and in different places. Their feast day is celebrated on February 14th. The first recorded connection between Saint Valentine's Day and romance occurs in Geoffrey Chaucer's 1382 poem titled "Parlement of Foules." It may have been inspired by a remnant of an older pagan fertility or marriage festival near the saints' feast day.

Popularity: top 1000 ↑

Related names:

Valentin – top 1000 →

Valentine – ♂♀ endangered →

Vito

Origin: Italian form of Vitus, Latin meaning "life."

Significance: Vitus was martyred under the emperor Diocletian in 303. He was 12-13 years old at the time.

Popularity: endangered →

Xander

Origin: short form of Alexander, Greek meaning "defender of men."

Significance: see Alexander.

Popularity: top 500 ↑

Spelling variations: *Zander*

Chapter 10: Saints

As you look through the names in this chapter, keep in mind that I wrote this book to help Christian couples find baby names. I didn't think it would be helpful to list every saint's name that's ever been. After all, no American parent has ever named a little boy Austriclinian or a little girl Cunegundes—two of the many never-used names I've seen in other Christian baby name books. Rather, my goal is to provide a comprehensive list of the Christian names currently used in the US. I've tried to give a general sense of the history of each name, together with its meaning and popularity.

Santino

Origin: diminutive of *santo*, "saint" in several Romance languages.

Significance: "saint" is an official title given by the Church in memory of those whose actions have demonstrated extraordinary holiness.

Popularity: top 1000 ↑

Related names:

Santos – "saint" in several Romance languages – top 1000 →

Santi – diminutive of Santino – endangered ↑

Saint – English form – endangered ↑

Sonny

Origin: nickname for Santino, an Italian diminutive of santo, "saint."

Significance: see Santino.

Popularity: top 1000 →

The Church to 500 AD

Ambrose

Origin: Greek meaning "immortal."

Significance: one of the four doctors of the Church. He is particularly known for fighting against Arianism— a theology that subordinates the son of God to God the father.

Popularity: endangered ↑

Related names:

Emrys – Welsh form – endangered ↑

Arsenio

Origin: Greek meaning "virile."

Significance: in his 30s, Arsenius the Great was a tutor in the Eastern Roman Empire to the emperor's sons. In those years, he lived a life of great luxury, but feeling that the lifestyle was bad for his soul, he gave up all worldly possessions for a life of extreme asceticism.

Popularity: endangered →

Atticus

Origin: Latin meaning "from Attica": Attica is a region in Greece that includes Athens.

Significance: a 5th century archbishop of Constantinople (now Istanbul).

Popularity: top 500 ↑

Aurelio

Origin: in several Romance languages, a form of Aurelius, Latin meaning "golden."

Significance: an influential Roman bishop who led several early councils on Christian doctrine.

Popularity: endangered →

Related names:

Aurelius – endangered ↑

Austin

Origin: contraction of Augustine, which is a variation of Augustus, meaning "exalted." The first emperor of Rome took *augustus* as a title, and it was used by succeeding emperors.

Significance: for Saint Augustine, one of the four doctors of the Church. His *City of God* and *Confessions of St. Augustine* have been extremely influential and are still widely read.

Popularity: top 100 ↓

Related names:

Augustine (AH-guss-teen) – diminutive of Augustus – top 1000 ↑

Agustin (uh-GUSS-tin) – variant of Augustine – top 1000 ↓

Cross-reference: Augustus is listed in the section titled "People and Places in the Life of Jesus" in chapter 7, "The New Testament" (page 110).

Basil

Origin: Greek meaning "king."

Significance: a bishop in the Eastern Roman Empire. He established forms of prayer and rules for monastic life, and fought against Arianism.

Popularity: endangered →

Blaine

Origin: variant spelling of Blane, Scotts Gaelic meaning "yellow," probably for a blond-haired child.

Significance: Saint Blane was a 6th century Scottish bishop with close ties to Ireland.

Popularity: top 1000 →

Brendan

Origin: from Brendanus, the Latinized form of the Irish name Bréanainn which comes from a Welsh word meaning "prince."

Significance: a 6th century Irish monk who founded several monasteries. He was also a famous navigator, particularly known for his legendary voyage to Isle of the Blessed, a phantom island in the North Atlantic Ocean.

Popularity: top 500 ↓

Related names: Note that Brandon and Branden are unrelated names that were first used as English last names about 1000 years after Saint Brendan lived.

Spelling variations: *Brenden, Brendon*

Bryce

Origin: from *ap Rhys*, meaning "son of Rhys" in Welsh; Rhys means "enthusiasm" in Welsh.

Significance: in the 5th century, an orphan raised by Saint Martin. Brice was exiled for seven years for immoral behavior. After a long period of repentance, he became a humble and pious man, and was made bishop of Tours, now in France.

Popularity: top 500 ↓

Related names:

Pryce – endangered ↑

Spelling variations: *Brice*

Clement

Origin: Latin meaning "gentle."

Significance: a companion of Peter and Paul. He was ordained bishop by Peter and later became the fourth pope.

Popularity: endangered →

Colin

Origin: Gaelic diminutive of Nicholas.

Significance: see Nicholas.

Popularity: top 500 ↓

Spelling variations: *Collin*

Conan

Origin: Gaelic meaning "little warrior."

Significance: there are several saints named Conan, the best-known of whom was a 7th century bishop of the Isle of Man.

Popularity: endangered ↑

Constantine

Origin: Latin meaning "constant, steadfast."

Significance: the first Christian emperor of the Roman Empire. In 313 he issued an edict that allowed for freedom of religion, ending the persecution of Christians.

Popularity: uncommon ↑

Related names:

Konstantinos – endangered →

Cornelius

Origin: a prestigious Roman family name.

Significance: pope from 251-253, a time when there was significant disagreement within the church regarding Christians who had stopped practicing the religion during a period of Roman persecution. Cornelius led the majority in being forgiving.

Popularity: uncommon ↓

Cross-reference: Cornelius was the name of the first Gentile convert, so it is also listed in chapter 7 (page 111).

Cyril

Origin: Greek meaning "lordly."

Significance: there were two early doctors of the Church named Cyril: Cyril of Jerusalem (313-386) and Cyril of Alexandria (376-444).

Popularity: endangered →

Cross-reference: Cyril is also the name of several important figures of the medieval Eastern Church. See "Saints of the Middle Ages" later in this chapter for more information (page 144).

Declan

Origin: English form of Deaglan, Irish Gaelic possibly meaning "full of goodness."

Significance: in the 5th century, he was a member of an Irish royal dynasty. He was ordained in Rome and returned to Ireland where he founded a monastery and converted others to his faith.

Popularity: top 500 ↑

Elian

Origin: ultimately Greek meaning "sun." It comes from the Roman family name Aelianus.

Significance: an early Roman missionary to Wales.

Popularity: top 1000 ↑

Elvis

Origin: English form of Ailbe, Irish Gaelic meaning "white."

Significance: Saint Ailbe was an influential 6th century Irish bishop who founded a monastery and diocese in southern Ireland. He is one of the patron saints of Ireland.

Popularity: uncommon ↓

Hilario

Origin: Iberian form of Hilarius, Latin meaning "cheerful."

Significance: As pope from 461-468, Hilarius worked to strengthen the church and the papacy.

Popularity: endangered ↓

Jerome

Origin: Greek meaning "sacred name."

Significance: one of the four doctors of the Church. He established forms of worship, wrote commentaries on scripture, and translated the Bible into Latin.

Popularity: top 1000 ↓

Julian

Origin: from Julia, a Roman family name.

Significance: Julius was a 4th century bishop of Rome who claimed that the authority of the Roman bishopric was greater than that of any other. He also established December 25th as Christmas day.

Popularity: top 100 ↑

Related names:

Julius – Roman – top 500 →

Julio – Spanish – top 500 ↓

Cross-reference: Julian and Julius are both listed in chapter 9 (page 132).

Leo

Origin: ultimately from Greek meaning "lion."

Significance: the name of thirteen popes, the first being Saint Leo the Great, who was pope from 440-461.

Popularity: top 100 ↑

Related names:

Leon – top 500 ↑

Leonel – top 500 →

Cross-reference: Leo, Leon, and Leonel are also be forms of Leo and are listed in chapter 9 (page 133).

Linus

Origin: a figure from Greek mythology.

Significance: the second pope, following Peter.

Popularity: uncommon ↑

Martin

Origin: from the Roman family name Martinus.

Significance: there have been seven saints named Martin, the earliest and best-known of whom was Martin of Tours, a 4th century French bishop who was a great early missionary.

Popularity: top 500 ↓

Related names:

Marty – diminutive – endangered →

Martino – Italian – endangered →

Cross-reference: Martin is also listed in chapter 11, "Protestant Leaders" (page 157).

Nicholas

Origin: Greek meaning "victory of the people."

Significance: a Greek bishop during the reign of Constantine I, a time of active efforts to unify the church. Nicholas was, of course, known for secretly giving gifts to those in need.

Popularity: top 100 ↓

Related names:

Nixon – a last name meaning "Nick's son" – top 1000 ↑

Nikolai – East Slavic – top 1000 ↑

Nikola – West Slavic. Traditionally a boys' name, but it is also used in the US for girls, though the name is rare for both boys and girls. – uncommon ↑

Nick – English short form – uncommon →

Klaus – German short form – endangered →

Spelling variations: *Nicolas, Nikolas, Nickolas*

Nico

Origin: a short form of Nicholas used in many languages.

Significance: see Nicholas.

Popularity: top 500 ↑

Spelling variations: *Niko*

Patrick

Origin: from Latin meaning "patrician."

Significance: a Romano-British missionary who was an important figure in the Christianization of Ireland. He is one of the island-nation's patron saints.

Popularity: top 500 ↓

Related names:

Patricio – used in several Romance languages – endangered →

Patterson – a last name meaning "Patrick's son" – endangered →

Padraig (PAW-drig) – Irish form – endangered →

Sylvester

Origin: Latin meaning "from the forest."

Significance: the name of three popes, including Sylvester I, who baptized Constantine I, the first Christian emperor of the Roman Empire.

Popularity: endangered →

Urban

Origin: Latin meaning "a person who lives in a city."

Significance: the name of eight popes, the first of whom was bishop of Rome from 222-230.

Popularity: endangered →

Saints of the Middle Ages

Aiden

Origin: variant spelling of Aidan, the English form of the Gaelic name Aodhan, itself a diminutive of Aodh, Celtic meaning "fire."

Significance: in the 7th century, an Irish monk and missionary. After the fall of the Roman Empire, England generally fell back into paganism. Aiden helped to re-establish Christianity.

Popularity: top 100 ↓

Spelling variations: *Ayden, Aidan, Aden, Aydan, Aydin, Aidyn, Aaden*

Alan

Origin: a Celtic name. Most popular sources give the meaning as "little rock," though this is not certain.

Significance: there have been three saints named Alan, the most well-know of whom is Alanus de Rupe (1428-1475). He was a strong supporter of the Rosary, and its use increased because of his preaching and his writings.

Popularity: top 500 →

Spelling variations: *Allen, Allan*

Albert

Origin: Germanic meaning "bright nobility."

Significance: there have been several saints named Albert: the earliest was born into the family of one of England's many 8th century kings and became a monk and missionary. He strengthened Christianity in Ireland, Holland, and Germany. The most famous of the saints named Albert was Albertus Magnus, the German philosopher and theologian.

Popularity: top 500 ↓

Related names:

Alberto – top 1000 ↓

Alexis

Origin: Greek meaning "protector, defender."

Significance: a noble Roman of the 5th century Eastern Roman Empire. Alexis left his home and family on his wedding day to live a life of poverty and penance.

Popularity: ♂♀ top 500 ↓

Related names:

Alex – top 500 ↓

Alessio – Italian – endangered ↑

Lex – endangered →

Alexi – endangered ↓

Alfred

Origin: Germanic meaning "elf counsel."

Significance: the great king of 9th century England who promoted literacy and learning in England. He founded two monasteries and, when there were not enough English monks to populate them, brought over monks from other countries.

Popularity: top 1000 →

Related names:

Alfredo – used in several Romance languages – top 1000 ↓

Ansel

Origin: short form of Anselm, Germanic meaning "protected by god."

Significance: Anselm of Canterbury (1033-1109), an influential philosopher and theologian, is a doctor of the Church. He was a Benedictine monk who became archbishop of Canterbury.

Popularity: uncommon ↑

Anthony

Origin: from Antonius, an ancient Roman family name. The English *th* was added during the Renaissance in a mistaken belief that the name was related to the Greek word *anthos*, meaning "flower."

Significance: Saint Anthony spent years living an ascetic life in the desert, and he inspired many to follow his example. He is considered the "father of monasticism."

Popularity: top 100 ↓

Related names:

Antonio – used in several Romance languages – top 500 ↓

Tony – short form – top 500 ↓

Anton – Germanic and Slavic – top 1000 →

Antoine – French – uncommon ↓

Deanthony – son of Anthony – endangered →

Marcanthony – endangered ↓

Marcoantonio – endangered ↓

Armando

Origin: in several Romance languages, a form of Herman, Germanic meaning "army man."

Significance: Hermann Joseph was a German monk who wrote about the transformation of the soul.

Popularity: top 500 ↓

Related names:

Armani – Italian – top 500 ↑

Arman – variation – uncommon →

German – Spanish and Slavic – uncommon →

Armand – French – endangered ↓

Herman – English – endangered ↓

Arnold

Origin: Germanic meaning "eagle-power."

Significance: an 11th century Belgian bishop. He is the patron saint of beer brewers and encouraged the drinking of beer, which was safer than the contaminated water of his time.

Popularity: endangered ↓

Related names:

Arnoldo – used in several Romance languages – endangered ↓

Avery

Origin: French form of Alfred, Germanic meaning "elf counsel."

Significance: see Alfred.

Popularity: top 500 ↑

Barrett

Origin: Irish form of Barnard, Germanic meaning "hardy as a bear."

Significance: Bernard was a 12th century French abbot. He worked for years to reunite Europe after it had been divided over the succession of the pope.

Popularity: top 500 ↑

Related names:

Bernard – uncommon →

Bernardo – uncommon →

Beckett

Origin: traditionally a last name with two possible sources: 1) It was sometimes given as a diminutive of a word related to beak, for someone with a big nose. 2) Beckett could also refer to someone who lived at a bee cot. (A cottage in the Middle Ages was a small, single-family farm.)

Significance: Thomas Beckett was an archbishop of Canterbury who resisted the efforts of Henry II to weaken the relationship between the English church and Rome, leading to his assassination and status as a martyr.

Popularity: top 500 ↑

Benedict

Origin: Latin meaning "blessed."

Significance: in the 6th century, he founded many communities for monks in Italy. He also established rules for their behavior that influenced the course of monasticism.

Popularity: uncommon →

Related names:

Bennett – English diminutive, traditionally a last name – top 500 ↑

Benson – an English last name meaning "Ben's son" – top 1000 ↑

Ben – short form of Benedict and Bennett – top 1000 →

Benito – Italian diminutive – uncommon →

Benicio – Spanish diminutive – endangered ↑

Boris

Origin: Slavic meaning "fight."

Significance: there are two saints named Boris: 1) The earliest was king of Bulgaria at the time of its conversion to Christianity. He helped bring Christianity to Slavic peoples. 2) The 11th century Saint Boris was a victim of political intrigue. With his brother Gleb, he was the first Rus saint.

Popularity: endangered →

Bruno

Origin: Germanic meaning "brown."

Significance: 11th century German monk, teacher, and founder of the Carthusian Order, an (oxymoronic) community of hermits.

Popularity: top 1000 ↑

Callum (KAL-uhm)

Origin: Scottish form of Columba, a Latin name meaning "dove."

Significance: there are a great many saints named Columba or some variation of the name. The best-known of these saints was an Irish abbot and missionary whose work in Scotland was important in converting the country to Christianity. He is a patron saint of Scotland.

Popularity: top 1000 ↑

Related names:

Colm – Irish – endangered →

Carlos

Origin: Iberian form of Carl, Germanic meaning "man," with the connotation "common man" or "freeman."

Significance: see Charles.

Popularity: top 500 ↓

Related names:

    Carl – Germanic – top 1000 ↓

    Carlo – Italian – uncommon →

    Carlito – diminutive – endangered →

    Decarlos – an Italian last name meaning "of Carlos" – endangered →

    Carlson – an English last name meaning "Carl's son" – endangered →

    Carlton – an English last name meaning "Carl's settlement" – endangered ↓

Chad

Origin: from Ceadda, an Anglo-Saxon name that probably includes the Welsh element *cad*, meaning "battle."

Significance: 7th century English bishop whose work strengthened the uniquely British form of the Church that developed in the north of Great Britain.

Popularity: top 1000 ↓

Charles

Origin: French form of Carl, Germanic meaning "man," with the connotation "common man" or "freeman."

Significance: there have been many saints named Charles (or a variation of the name). The earliest and best-known of these saints is Charlemagne, the first Holy Roman emperor.

Popularity: top 100 →

Related names:

    Charlie – English diminutive. Traditionally a boys' name, Charlie is now almost as popular for girls as it is for boys – ♂♀ top 500 ↑

Claudio

Origin: masculine form of Claudia, an imperial Roman family name.

Significance: Claudius of Besançon was a 7th century French bishop.

Popularity: endangered ↓

Related names:

    Claude – French – endangered ↓

Coleman

Origin: English name used as an equivalent to the Gaelic name Callum, which comes from Columba, a Latin name meaning "dove." The English name originally meant "coal worker."

Significance: see Callum.

Popularity: top 1000 ↓

Conrad

Origin: Germanic meaning "bold council."

Significance: there were three medieval saints named Conrad. The first, Conrad of Constance (900-975) was a German bishop who came from a noble and powerful family.

Popularity: top 1000 ↑

Related names:

    Cord – Germanic contraction – endangered →

Cyril

Origin: Greek meaning "lordly."

Significance: in the Eastern Orthodox Church, Cyril has been the name of saints, popes, and patriarchs. Among the most well-known was a 9th century Macedonian missionary. With his brother, Methodius, he developed the precursor to the Cyrillic alphabet in order to translate the Bible into Slavic.

Popularity: endangered →

Cross-reference: Cyril is also listed in the previous section (page 138).

Daylen

Origin: variant spelling of Dallan, Irish Gaelic meaning "little blind one." It was a nickname given to Dallan Forgaill because he so damaged his eyesight by constant studying.

Significance: Dallan Forgaill was an Irish scholar and poet, particularly known for his eulogies of Irish saints.

Popularity: uncommon →

Dominic

Origin: from *dies Dominica*, Latin for "Sunday," directly translated as "day of the Lord." The name was often given to children born on Sunday.

Significance: a Spanish priest who, in 1215, founded the Dominican Order, an intellectual order dedicated to learning and teaching.

Popularity: top 100 ↑

Related names:

Domingo – Iberian – endangered ↓

Domenico – Italian – endangered →

Spelling variations: *Dominick, Dominik*

Donald

Origin: Gaelic meaning "ruler of the world."

Significance: 7th century Scottish saint and father of the Nine Maidens. His daughters all entered a monastery after his death.

Popularity: top 500 ↓

Related names:

Don – uncommon →

Donny – endangered →

Edgar

Origin: Germanic meaning "prosperous spear."

Significance: a 10th century English king who brought Benedictine rule back to English monasteries.

Popularity: top 500 ↓

Edmund

Origin: Germanic meaning "prosperous protector."

Significance: there have been six saints named Edmund. The earliest was a 9th century king of south-east England who was martyred by Viking raiders when he refused to renounce Christianity.

Popularity: uncommon ↑

Edward

Origin: Germanic meaning "prosperous strength."

Significance: there are two saints named Edward: 1) Edward the Martyr was a 10th century king, murdered through the political machinations of his stepmother. 2) Edward the Confessor was an 11th century English king, a truly pious man and the last of the Anglo-Saxon kings.

Popularity: top 500 →

Related names:

Edison – an English last name – top 500 ↑

Eduardo – used in several Romance languages – top 500 ↓

Eddie – English diminutive – top 1000 ↓

Edwin

Origin: Germanic meaning "prosperous friend."

Significance: a king of northern England who converted in 627. The conversion of kings was important because the conversion of their subjects usually followed.

Popularity: top 500 ↓

Enrique (ahn-REE-keh)

Origin: Spanish form of Henry, Germanic meaning "home ruler."

Significance: see Henry.

Popularity: top 500 ↓

Eric

Origin: Germanic meaning "one ruler."

Significance: a 12th century Swedish king who strengthened Christianity in Sweden and worked to convert Finland.

Popularity: top 500 ↓

Spelling variations: *Erick, Erik*

Francis

Origin: short form of Francesco, Italian meaning "Frenchman." It was a nickname for Saint Francis of Assisi given to him by his father, who was in France on business when his son was born. His given name was Giovanni.

Significance: St. Francis Xavier was an effective preacher and missionary who founded three religious orders, including the extraordinarily influential Third Order of St. Francis.

Popularity: used for both boys and girls in fairly similar numbers; however, *Francis* is the usual spelling for boys and *Frances* is the usual spelling for girls. – ♂♀ top 500 ↑

Related names:

Francisco – Iberian form of Francesco – top 500 ↓

Frank – commonly used as a short from of Francis, though the name originally referred to the Franks (see page 127) – top 500 ↓

Frankie – diminutive of Frank – top 1000 →

Franco – contracted form of Francesco – top 1000 →

Francesco – original form of the nickname – uncommon →

Franz – German short form of Francis – endangered →

Frederick

Origin: Germanic meaning "peaceful ruler."

Significance: a well-educated and pious man who became bishop of Utrecht (now in Netherlands) in the 9th century.

Popularity: top 500 →

Related names:

Fred – short form – uncommon →

Freddy – English diminutive – uncommon ↓

Federico – Spanish and Italian – endangered →

Friedrich – German – endangered →

Fritz – German diminutive – endangered →

Garrett

Origin: Irish form of Gerald, Germanic meaning "spear hardy."

Significance: there have been seven saints named Gerald, most of whom were French. The earliest was Gerald of Mayo, a 7th century English monk who founded a monastery in County Mayo, Ireland, and became its abbot.

Popularity: top 500 ↓

Related names:

Jarrett – uncommon ↓

Gerardo

Origin: Spanish form of Gerald, Germanic meaning "spear hardy."

Significance: see Garrett.

Popularity: top 500 ↓

Related names:

Gerald – top 1000 ↓

Garrison – uncommon →

Gilbert

Origin: Germanic meaning "bright pledge." In the Middle Ages, children were often sent to live with rival tribes as pledges of peace.

Significance: 12th century English priest and founder of the Gilbertines, an English order that included twenty-six religious communities and endured for five centuries, until the dissolution of the monasteries under Henry VIII.

Popularity: top 1000 ↓

Related names:

Gilberto – used in several Romance languages – uncommon ↓

Gil – endangered →

Gregory

Origin: ultimately Greek meaning "watchful, alert."

Significance: Pope Gregory I is considered "the father of Christian worship" for the many changes he made to the traditional forms and order of the liturgy. The established form of chants, for example, are attributed to him and were named for him—the Gregorian chants.

Popularity: top 500 ↓

Related names:

Greg – short form – endangered ↓

Gregorio – used in several Romance languages – endangered ↓

Guillermo

Origin: Spanish form of William, Germanic meaning "intending to protect."

Significance: see William.

Popularity: top 1000 ↓

Related names:

Guilherme – endangered ↓

Guy

Origin: French form of Guido, a Latin variation of Wido. Wido is a Germanic short form of names starting with *widu*, meaning "wood, forest."

Significance: there were two saints named Guy: 1) Guy of Anderlecht was a poor Belgian man famous for his pilgrimages to Rome and Jerusalem. 2) Guy of Pomposa was from a wealthy Italian family but gave up his worldly life to become a monk. He was an abbot and founder of a new monastery.

Popularity: uncommon →

Harold

Origin: Germanic meaning "army power."

Significance: in 12th century England, one of several young boys who, at the time, were believed to have been killed by Jews and so are considered martyrs.

Popularity: top 1000 ↓

Harrison

Origin: an English last name meaning "Harry's son." *Harry* is a spelling that reflects the medieval English pronunciation of Henry, Germanic meaning "home ruler."

Significance: see Henry.

Popularity: 500 ↑

Related names:

Harry – top 1000 →

Harris – uncommon →

Henry

Origin: Germanic meaning "home ruler."

Significance: there were three saints named Henry: 1) Henry II who was

Holy Roman emperor from 1014-1024; 2) a 12th century English bishop who is believed to have been a missionary to Finland; 3) Henry of Cocket, a 12th century Danish hermit.

Popularity: top 100 ↑

Related names:

Hendrix – English spelling of a Germanic form – top 1000 ↑

Henrik – Germanic – top 1000 ↑

Hendrick – Germanic – endangered ↑

Heriberto

Origin: Iberian form of Herbert, Germanic meaning "army bright," implying an illustrious warrior.

Significance: there are two saints named Herbert: 1) Herbert of Derwentwater, a 7th century English hermit; 2) a French archbishop of Tours.

Popularity: endangered ↓

Related names:

Herbert – English – endangered ↓

Hernan

Origin: Spanish short form of Fernando, Germanic of uncertain meaning. The most straightforward meaning is "prepared to journey." Other possibilities are: "prepared for peace," "brave journey," and "brave peace."

Significance: a 13th century Castilian king. He re-conquered vast territories of Moorish occupied Spain, returning them to Christian rule.

Popularity: endangered ↓

Related names:

Ferdinand – endangered →

Hernando – endangered →

Hilario

Origin: Spanish form of Hilarius, Latin meaning "cheerful."

Significance: Hilarius was pope from 461-468, during which time he worked to strengthen the church and the papacy.

Popularity: endangered →

Hugo

Origin: form of Hugh used in several Romance and Germanic languages. A short form of Germanic names starting with *hug*, meaning "spirit/heart."

Significance: there have been ten saints named Hugh, the earliest of whom was Hugh of Champagne, an 8th century French bishop.

Popularity: top 500 →

Related names:

Hugh – top 1000 ↑

Houston – top 1000 →

Hughes – endangered →

Huey – endangered →

Ignacio

Origin: Spanish form of Ignatius, from the Roman family name Egnacia.

Significance: Ignatius of Loyola founded the Society of Jesus (the Jesuit order).

Popularity: uncommon ↓

Related names:

Ignatius – English – endangered ↑

Cross-reference: Ignatius is also the name of a disciple of the apostle John. For more information see chapter 9, "Early Martyrs" (page 131).

Isidro

Origin: the Spanish form of Isidoros, Greek meaning "gift of Isis."

Significance: there are two Spanish saints named Isidro: 1) a 6th century scholar and archbishop of Seville; 2) an 11th century farmer who is known for his kindness toward animals.

Popularity: endangered ↓

Ivo

Origin: short form of Germanic names staring with *iv*, meaning "yew tree."

Significance: there have been three saints named Ivo: 1) The earliest, also called Saint Ives, was an 11th century English bishop who lived in Cornwall. 2) Saint Ivo of Chartre was an 11th century French bishop. 3) Saint Ivo of Kermartin was a 12th century French priest who is much-loved for having been a defender of the poor and sick.

Popularity: endangered →

Related names:

Yves – French – endangered →

Javier

Origin: the name of the town in which Saint Francis was born. Like Xavier, it comes from the Basque word *etxeberri*, meaning "new house."

Significance: see Francis.

Popularity: top 500 ↓

Javion

Origin: variation of Javier, the name of the town in which Saint Francis was born.

Significance: see Francis.

Popularity: top 1000 →

Spelling variations: *Jayvion*

Jermaine

Origin: alternate spelling of Germain, ultimately Latin meaning "brother."

Significance: bishop of Paris from 555. He founded the Abbey of Saint-Germain-des-Prés in Paris.

Popularity: top 1000 ↓

Jerry

Origin: diminutive of Jarret, a form of Garrett, the Irish form of Gerald, Germanic meaning "spear hardy."

Significance: see Garrett.

Popularity: top 500 ↓

Related names:

Jarrett – uncommon ↓

Kenneth

Origin: the English form of two different Celtic names: 1) Cainnech meaning "handsome"; 2) Cenydd, which comes from *aidhu*, meaning "fire."

Significance: there were two 6th century saints named Kenneth: 1) Cainnech of Aghaboe, an Irish missionary; 2) Saint Cenydd, a Welsh hermit.

Popularity: top 500 ↓

Related names:

Kenny – diminutive – top 1000 ↓

Ken – short form – endangered →

Kevin

Origin: English form of the Gaelic name Caoimhin, meaning "well born."

Significance: Kevin of Glendalough (498-618) was an Irish holy man and hermit who founded a monastery at Glendalough. The monastery was influential through the 13th century.

Popularity: top 100 ↓

Kian (KEE-in)

Origin: variant spelling of Cian, Irish Gaelic meaning "ancient." The letter *k* is not used in the Irish alphabet.

Significance: a 6th century Welsh saint about whom little is known.

Popularity: top 500 ↑

Kieran

Origin: English spelling of the Celtic name Ciaran, meaning "dark."

Significance: there have been twenty-six Irish saints named Ciaran. The earliest was Ciaran of Saigir (501-530), an Irish nobleman and bishop who founded a monastery in central Ireland.

Popularity: top 1000 →

Killian

Origin: English spelling of the Celtic name Cillian, probably related to a word meaning "church," but possibly related to a word meaning "struggle, strife."

Significance: there are two Irish saints named Killian: 1) The earliest was a 7th century abbot who is remembered for having written a biography of Saint Brigid. 2) The best known of the saints Killian also lived in the 7th century. He was a missionary to what is now Germany, where he and his companions converted many people.

Popularity: top 1000 ↑

Landry

Origin: from the Germanic name Landric, meaning "land-power."

Significance: the name of two French bishops of the early Middle Ages.

Popularity: top 1000 ↑

Leander

Origin: Greek meaning "lion of the people."

Significance: a 6th century Spanish bishop who converted to Christianity two Germanic kings of the Iberian Peninsula. The conversion of kings was important because their subjects were usually converted soon after.

Popularity: uncommon ↑

Ledger

Origin: from Leodegar, a Germanic name meaning "tribe's spear."

Significance: Leodegar was an energetic French bishop who worked to improve and enlarge churches, charitable institutions, and public buildings. He was murdered 679 as a result of court intrigue and is considered a martyr.

Popularity: endangered ↑

Leonardo

Origin: Latin-Germanic blend meaning "hardy as a lion": Latin *leo*, "lion" + Germanic *heard*, "hardy."

Significance: a 6th century noble in the court of the first French king, Clovis I. Leonard converted with the king on Christmas day and later became a monk and a hermit.

Popularity: top 500 ↑

Related names:

Leonard – English and French – top 1000 →

Lenny – English diminutive – endangered →

Len – short form – endangered →

Leopold

Origin: Germanic meaning "bold among the people."

Significance: a 12th century Austrian ruler who founded several monasteries. He is one of the patron saints of Austria.

Popularity: endangered ↑

Related names:

Leopoldo – used in several Romance languages – endangered ↓

Liam

Origin: Irish short form of William, Germanic meaning "intending to protect."

Significance: see William.

Popularity: top 10 ↑

Louis (LU-iss)

Origin: Germanic meaning "famous fighter."

Significance: there have been sixteen saints named Louis, the earliest of whom was Louis IX, king of France.

Popularity: top 500 ↑

Related names:

Louie – English diminutive – uncommon ↑

Lou – short form – endangered ↑

Aloysius (al-o-WISH-uhs) – Occitan – endangered →

Spelling variations: *Lewis*

Luis (lu-EES)

Origin: Spanish form of Louis, Germanic meaning "famous fighter."

Significance: see Louis.

Popularity: top 100 ↓

Related names:

Gino – Italian diminutive of several names, including Luigi – top 1000 →

Luigi – Italian – endangered →

Luiz – Portuguese – endangered ↓

Luisangel – endangered ↓

Maximus

Origin: Latin meaning "greatest."

Significance: 7ᵗʰ century monk and theologian who successfully defended the belief that Jesus had both human and divine will, opposing a competing view that Jesus had only divine will.

Popularity: top 500 ↑

Related names:

Max – short form – top 500 →

Maxim – Slavic – top 1000 →

Maximo – Spanish – top 1000 →

Massimo – Italian – uncommon →

Maximos – Greek – endangered ↓

Rainer

Origin: Germanic meaning "counselled army."

Significance: there were at least four medieval saints named Raynerius. The most well-known came from Pisa, Italy, and is a patron saint of that city. He began as a traveling mistral who led a life of loose morals, but he became an extremely devout and austere monk.

Popularity: endangered →

Raul

Origin: Spanish form of Rodulf, Germanic meaning "wolf council."

Significance: the 9ᵗʰ century French saint Rodulf was an archbishop and influential monastic reformer.

Popularity: top 500 ↓

Related names:

Ralph – English – uncommon ↓

Rafe (RAYF) – modern spelling of the medieval English pronunciation of Ralph – endangered →

Raymond

Origin: Germanic meaning "protective counsel."

Significance: there have been two saints named Raymond, both of whom were Spanish monks: 1) Raymond of Penyafort (c. 1175-1275) was a Dominican who worked to collect and unify published writings on Church law. His work was part of the Catholic Church's cannon laws until the 20ᵗʰ century. 2) Raymond Nonnatus (1204-1240) was a member of Mercedarians, an order that rescued Christians who had been enslaved by the Moors.

Popularity: top 500 ↓

Related names:

Ray – short form – top 1000 →

Ramon – Spanish – top 1000 ↓

Raymundo – Iberian – endangered ↓

Redmond – Irish – endangered ↑

Remy

Origin: short form of the Latin name Remigius, meaning "oarsman."

Significance: Saint Remigius was a French bishop who baptized Clovis, the king of the Franks, on Christmas day, 496. Clovis's conversion eventually led all of France to become Catholic.

Popularity: traditionally a boys' name, but now slightly more popular for girls than boys. The spelling *Remi* is used almost exclusively for girls, while *Remy* is slightly more popular for boys. – ♂♀ top 1000 ↑

Ricardo

Origin: Iberian form of Richard, Germanic meaning "hardy ruler."

Significance: see Richard.

Popularity: top 500 ↓

Related names:

Rico – contraction – uncommon →

Richard

Origin: Germanic meaning "hardy ruler."

Significance: there have been eighteen saints named Richard. The earliest was Richard the Pilgrim, a king in what is now southern England. He died on pilgrimage to Rome in the 8th century.

Popularity: top 500 ↓

Related names:

Ricky – diminutive – top 1000 ↓

Rick – short form – endangered ↓

Rich – short form – endangered →

Richie – diminutive – endangered →

Dixon – an English last name meaning "Dick's son." Dick is an old nickname for Richard. In England, rhyming with the first syllable of a name was once a popular way to create nicknames. – endangered →

Ryker – a Dutch last name meaning "Rick's son" – top 500 ↑

Robert

Origin: Germanic meaning "bright fame."

Significance: there were two medieval saints named Robert: 1) Robert of Molesme (1029-1111) was a French abbot who helped found the Cistercian order. 2) Robert of Newminister (1100-1159) was an English abbot who established a monastery in northern England and encouraged the founding of other monasteries into central England.

Popularity: top 100 ↓

Related names:

Roberto – top 500 ↓

Bobby – top 1000 ↓

Bob – endangered →

Robin – uncommon →

Robbie – endangered →

Rob – endangered →

Robinson – endangered ↑

Robson – endangered →

Robertson– endangered →

Rocco

Origin: Italian form of Roch, a Germanic name of uncertain meaning.

Significance: Roch was a 14th century French saint who traveled to Italy, where he cared for victims of the plague, miraculously curing many sufferers.

Popularity: top 500 →

Related names:

Rocky – English diminutive – top 1000 →

Rock – English – endangered →

Roque – Iberian – endangered →

Rodrigo

Origin: Spanish form of Roderick, Germanic meaning "famous ruler."

Significance: Saint Roderick was one of the 48 Martyrs of Cordoba who was killed in the 9th century during the Moorish occupation of Spain.

Popularity: endangered ↓

Related names:

Roderick – English – uncommon ↓

Roger

Origin: Germanic meaning "famous spear."

Significance: there are three saints named Roger: 1) Roger of Cannae, an 11th century Italian bishop; 2) Roger of Todi, a 13th century Franciscan monk and a companion of Saint Francis; 3) Roger Niger, a 13th century bishop of London.

Popularity: top 1000 ↓

Related names:

Rogers – a Welsh last name meaning "Roger's son" – endangered →

Roland

Origin: Germanic meaning "famous land."

Significance: a 12th century British monk who became abbot of a monastery in France.

Popularity: endangered ↑

Ronald

Origin: Germanic meaning "rules with council."

Significance: Saint Ronald (Rognvald Kale Kolsson) was a Norwegian earl of the Orkney Islands (now a part of Scotland) who had a great cathedral built there. He is particularly known for a pilgrimage to the Holy Land.

Popularity: top 500 ↓

Related names:

Ronaldo – Portuguese – uncommon ↓

Ronny – English diminutive – endangered →

Ron – short form – endangered →

Ronan

Origin: Celtic meaning "little seal."

Significance: a 6th century Irish bishop who exiled himself to Brittany (in north-western France) and became a hermit. The place where he founded his hermitage is now a village called Locronan, meaning "hermitage of Ronan."

Popularity: top 500 ↑

Spelling variations: *Ronin*

Rowan

Origin: English spelling of Ruadhan, Gaelic meaning "little red."

Significance: Ruadhan of Lorrha was a 6th century Irish prophet who founded a monastery, of which he was the abbot, in central Ireland.

Popularity: top 500 ↑

Rudolph

Origin: Germanic meaning "wolf shield."

Significance: an 11th century Italian bishop.

Popularity: endangered →

Related names:

Rodolfo – used in several Romance languages – endangered ↓

Rudy – English diminutive – endangered ↓

Rupert

Origin: Low German form of Robert, a Germanic name meaning "bright fame."

Significance: there are two saints named Rupert: 1) Rupert of Salzburg (660-710) was a German bishop who founded the city of Salzburg. 2) Rupert of Bingen (712-732) died when he was twenty years old, having completed a pilgrimage to Rome and, with his mother, built churches and homes to care for the sick and poor.

Popularity: endangered →

Sergio

Origin: from of Sergia, a patrician Roman family name. This form is used in Spain and Italy.

Significance: Sergius of Radonezh (1214-1392) was Russian ascetic who founded several monasteries, with many more being established by his followers.

Popularity: top 500 ↓

Related names:

Sergey – Slavic – endangered →

Serge – French – endangered →

Thomas

Origin: Aramaic meaning "twin."

Significance: there were two medieval saints named Thomas: 1) Thomas Becket was an archbishop of Canterbury who resisted the efforts of King Henry II to weaken the relationship between the English Church and Rome, leading to his assassination and status as a martyr. 2) Thomas Aquinas was a highly influential 13th century priest, philosopher, and theologian.

Popularity: top 100 ↓

Related names:

Tommy – top 1000 ↓

Tom – endangered ↓

Spelling variations: *Tomas*

Cross-reference: Thomas is also the name of one the Twelve Apostles and is included in the section titled "People and Places in the Life of Jesus" in chapter 2, "The New Testament" (page 115).

Vladimir

Origin: a Slavic name of Germanic origin, meaning "famous power."

Significance: a 10th century Slavic ruler who converted to Christianity and brought his new-found faith to his people.

Popularity: uncommon →

Related names:

Vlad – endangered →

Wendell

Origin: Germanic meaning "wanderer." It is also a variation of Vandal, the name of a medieval Germanic tribe.

Significance: a Germanic hermit who (oxymoronically) established a community of hermits in what is now Germany. The community grew to become a Benedictine Abbey, of which Wendell became the abbot.

Popularity: endangered →

William

Origin: Germanic meaning "intending to protect."

Significance: there have been thirty-five saints name William, the earliest of whom was William of Gellone. He was a French count and military leader who protected France against the invading Moors. In 804 he founded a monastery where he lived as a monk until his death.

Popularity: top 10 ↓

Related names:

Wilson – an English last name meaning "Will's son" – top 1000 →

Willie – diminutive – top 1000 ↓

Will – short form – top 1000 ↓

Bill – nickname for William. In England, rhyming with the first syllable of a name was once a popular way to create nicknames. – endangered →

Billie – diminutive of Bill – endangered →

Wilhelm – German – endangered →

Wolfgang

Origin: Germanic meaning "wolf path."

Significance: Wolfgang of Regensburg (934-994) was a German bishop, reformer, and the teacher of several influential men of his time.

Popularity: endangered ↑

Related names:

Wolf – endangered ↑

Xavier (ZAY-vee-er)

Origin: from the birthplace of Saint Francis, the Castle of Xavier in Javier,

Navarre, part of modern-day Spain. The place name comes from the Basque word *etxeberri*, meaning "new house."

Significance: see Francis.

Popularity: top 100 →

Related names:

Xavi – short form – uncommon →

Zavion – variation – uncommon →

Savion – variation – uncommon ↓

Spelling variations: *Zavier*

Later Saints

Guadalupe

Origin: Guadalupe is a province in Mexico.

Significance: the Virgin Mary is said to have appeared to a peasant in 16th century Guadalupe.

Popularity: ♀ endangered ↓

Oliver

Origin: though often given a Latin etymology related to olives, this name is more likely Germanic. Its meaning, however, in unknown.

Significance: Oliver Plunkett (1625-1681) was an Irish archbishop infamously executed as a result of the Popish Plot, a Protestant conspiracy to make it seem that English Catholics wanted to assassinate the King.

Popularity: top 100 ↑

Related names:

Ollie – endangered ↑

Chapter 11: Protestant Leaders

Calvin

Origin: English form of *chuavin*, French meaning "bald."

Significance: John Calvin (1509-1564) was an important figure in the Protestant Reformation. His work led to a branch of Protestant faith called Calvinism. Jean Chauvin is the original French form of the name.

Popularity: top 500 ↑

Related names:

Cal – uncommon →

Luther

Origin: Germanic meaning "people army."

Significance: Martin Luther (1483-1546) was an early leader of the Protestant Reformation. He was a German priest who disagreed with some of the Catholic Church's fundamental theology and practices.

Popularity: endangered →

Martin

Origin: short form of the Roman family name Martinus.

Significance: see Luther.

Popularity: top 500 ↓

Related names:

Marty – endangered ↓

Martino – endangered ↓

Cross-reference: Martin is also the name of several saints and is included in the section titled "The Church to 500 AD" in chapter 10, "Saints" (page 139).

Wesley

Origin: contracted form of Westley, meaning "west meadow."

Significance: John and Charles Wesley were English brothers whose theology gave rise to the Methodist Church.

Popularity: top 500 ↑

Index

A

Name	Page	Rank	Births	Gender
Aaron	98, 129	50	7334	boy
Aaron	11	5578	23	girl
Abbott	121	2563	47	boy
Abby	14	389	830	girl
Abdiel	94	859	255	boy
Abe	94	2306	56	boy
Abel	94	164	2551	boy
Abigail	14	8	11985	girl
Abilene	22	3302	48	girl
Abner	100	1016	198	boy
Abraham	94	180	2351	boy
Abram	94	377	823	boy
Absalom	101	10641	6	boy
Ace	126	379	818	boy
Adah	8	2378	76	girl
Adam	94	79	5293	boy
Adamary	35	7576	15	girl
Adán	94	373	829	boy
Adara	21	2555	68	girl
Addison	8	24	6950	girl
Adelaida	81	5268	25	girl
Adelaide	81	316	1040	girl
Adiel	100	1667	91	boy
Adina	14	1519	143	girl
Adora	37	3121	52	girl
Adria	66	2863	59	girl
Adrian	129	59	6659	boy
Adriana	66	177	1861	girl
Adriano	129	1875	77	boy
Adriel	14	3205	50	girl
Adrienne	66	811	339	girl

Name	Page	Rank	Births	Gender
Andreas	110	1338	128	boy
Andrés	110	222	1696	boy
Andrew	110	22	11069	boy
Andrew	22	9527	11	girl
Andriana	22	6187	20	girl
Andy	110	281	1263	boy
Angel	121	67	6255	boy
Angel	49	275	1179	girl
Angela	49	191	1722	girl
Angeles	49	3062	54	girl
Angelia	49	2725	63	girl
Angelic	49	4437	32	girl
Angelica	49	437	727	girl
Angelina	49	153	2105	girl
Angeline	49	847	323	girl
Angelique	49	413	768	girl
Angelita	49	4532	31	girl
Angelito	121	6280	13	boy
Angelo	121	315	1098	boy
Angelus	121	5969	14	boy
Angely	49	1445	155	girl
Angelyn	49	3305	48	girl
Angie	49	550	558	girl
Aniela	49	4341	33	girl
Anika	45	519	589	girl
Anita	45	1390	164	girl
Aniyah	45	226	1479	girl
Anna	45	34	5639	girl
Annabella	46, 82	256	1265	girl
Annabelle	46, 82	57	4324	girl
Annabeth	44, 47	1174	207	girl
Annaclaire	46	6682	18	girl
Annagrace	46, 51	3897	38	girl
Annakate	47	8460	13	girl

Name	Page	Rank	Births	Gender
Aurelio	137	1832	80	boy
Aurelius	137	2967	38	boy
Austin	137	66	6263	boy
Austyn	78	1063	240	girl
Avagrace	51	5003	27	girl
Avamarie	35	2221	84	girl
Avery	142	186	2269	boy
Axel	101	145	2777	boy
Ayah	14	1735	119	girl
Ayden	82	2308	79	girl
Azaria	17, 19	927	287	girl
Azariah	106, 108	838	264	boy
Azelie	82	14738	6	girl
Azeneth	8	2129	89	girl
Azriel	101	1797	82	boy
Azriella	14	10177	10	girl
Azrielle	14	10178	10	girl

B

Name	Page	Rank	Births	Gender
Baltazar	120	3136	35	boy
Barbara	67	863	315	girl
Barnabas	110	6292	13	boy
Barnaby	110	7552	10	boy
Barrett	142	346	950	boy
Bartholomew	110	7553	10	boy
Basil	137	2739	43	boy
Bastian	134	1374	123	boy
Beatrice	67	601	482	girl
Beatrix	67	1332	175	girl
Beatriz	67	1550	139	girl
Beautiful	60	3307	48	girl
Becca	11	3412	46	girl
Beckett	143	244	1511	boy
Beckett	82	2309	79	girl
Becky	11	3095	53	girl

Name	Page	Rank	Births	Gender
Belen	22, 37	996	263	girl
Belicia	42	7663	15	girl
Bella	42, 56, 60	70	4050	girl
Belladonna	60	6701	18	girl
Belle	42, 56, 60	1030	250	girl
Ben	94, 143	723	329	boy
Benaiah	101	1628	94	boy
Benedict	143	1281	137	boy
Benicio	143	1339	128	boy
Benito	143	1670	91	boy
Benjamin	94	12	13687	boy
Benji	94	2740	43	boy
Bennett	143	166	2525	boy
Bennett	82	1802	112	girl
Benny	94	1275	138	boy
Benson	143	526	524	boy
Berenice	55	2452	73	girl
Berit	83	10187	10	girl
Bernadette	91	1645	129	girl
Bernard	142	1173	157	boy
Bernardo	142	1482	108	boy
Bess	42	12029	8	girl
Bessie	42	9567	11	girl
Beth	8, 42	3526	44	girl
Bethany	22	393	824	girl
Bethel	8	2868	59	girl
Betsy	42	1621	131	girl
Bette	42	12030	8	girl
Bettina	42	9570	11	girl
Betty	42	1254	190	girl
Beulah	15, 49	9571	11	girl
Bianca	57	360	901	girl
Bibiana	77	5009	27	girl
Bill	156	2605	46	boy

Name	Page	Rank	Births	Gender
Cecilia	68	206	1623	girl
Cecily	68	1060	242	girl
Celeste	50	467	674	girl
Celestia	50	8516	13	girl
Celestial	50	13256	7	girl
Celestina	50	5154	26	girl
Celestine	50	6452	19	girl
Cesar	111	279	1279	boy
Chad	144	703	344	boy
Champ	127	3685	28	boy
Champion	127	4251	23	boy
Chantal	84	3127	52	girl
Charisma	60	2562	68	girl
Charity	57, 68	1057	243	girl
Charlene	84	1432	157	girl
Charles	144	51	7269	boy
Charles	84	7692	15	girl
Charlie	144	225	1670	boy
Charlie	84	229	1432	girl
Charlize	84	1007	258	girl
Charlotte	84	10	10048	girl
Chastity	57	5017	27	girl
Cherish	64	804	345	girl
Chevelle	42	1397	163	girl
Chevy	42	3581	43	girl
Chloe	23	18	8469	girl
Chris	122, 130	514	535	boy
Chrisette	50	3582	43	girl
Chrissy	50	3471	45	girl
Christabella	50	6455	19	girl
Christabelle	50	9618	11	girl
Christian	122	42	8388	boy
Christian	50	1611	132	girl
Christiana	50	1366	168	girl

Name	Page	Rank	Births	Gender
Christiano	122	2268	58	boy
Christina	50	326	1012	girl
Christine	50	689	407	girl
Christobal	122, 130	8862	8	boy
Christopher	122, 130	30	10278	boy
Christos	122	2834	41	boy
Christy	50	2203	85	girl
Ciara	88	673	418	girl
Cielo	50	1790	113	girl
Claire	84	44	4991	girl
Clara	84	108	2833	girl
Clarabelle	84	5796	22	girl
Clarice	84	3217	50	girl
Clarissa	84	765	362	girl
Clarita	84	12099	8	girl
Claude	144	2789	42	boy
Claudia	85	724	383	girl
Claudio	144	2269	58	boy
Clemence	78	14879	6	girl
Clement	138	2835	41	boy
Clementina	78	8084	14	girl
Clementine	78	943	283	girl
Cohen	98	342	961	boy
Coleman	144	950	220	boy
Colette	79	522	587	girl
Colin	138	140	2869	boy
Collins	79	838	327	girl
Colm	143	7596	10	boy
Conan	138	2651	45	boy
Concepción	33	13284	7	girl
Concetta	33	12102	8	girl
Connie	57	2499	71	girl
Conrad	144	649	402	boy
Constance	57	1599	133	girl

Name	Page	Rank	Births	Gender
Davey	101	5256	17	boy
Davi	101	2008	70	boy
David	101	18	12078	boy
Davida	15	7706	15	girl
Davina	15	1280	185	girl
Davis	101	446	660	boy
Dawson	101	320	1073	boy
Daylen	145	1209	150	boy
Daylin	85	3419	46	girl
Deacon	123	421	724	boy
Dean	123	221	1700	boy
Deandre	110	619	425	boy
Deangelo	121	968	215	boy
Deanthony	142	1952	73	boy
Debbie	12	3829	39	girl
Deborah	12	753	368	girl
Decarlos	144	7124	11	boy
Declan	138	122	3299	boy
Delilah	12	130	2496	girl
Demarcus	113	1004	203	boy
Demaria	30	9060	12	girl
Demetrius	130	692	357	boy
Denise	68	777	358	girl
Dennis	130	491	569	boy
Denny	130	2837	41	boy
Desi	123	5486	16	boy
Desi	50	6220	20	girl
Desiderio	123	10976	6	boy
Desire	50	2455	73	girl
Desirée	50	700	398	girl
Destiny	50	160	2043	girl
Didier	123	3084	36	boy
Diego	120	129	3154	boy
Dietrich	135	2331	55	boy

Name	Page	Rank	Births	Gender
Dimitri	130	882	244	boy
Dina	8	1512	144	girl
Dinah	8	3101	53	girl
Dixon	153	1935	74	boy
Dolly	68	5627	23	girl
Dolores	33	3644	42	girl
Domenico	145	2173	62	boy
Domingo	145	2294	57	boy
Dominic	145	69	6205	boy
Dominica	54, 85	7337	16	girl
Dominique	54, 85	1513	144	girl
Don	145	1466	110	boy
Donald	145	418	730	boy
Donatella	68	11139	9	girl
Donatello	130	3362	32	boy
Donato	130	3912	26	boy
Donna	33	1407	161	girl
Donny	145	2838	41	boy
Dorcas	28	5804	22	girl
Dorothea	68	5030	27	girl
Dorothy	68	731	380	girl
Dove	53	6222	20	girl
Dovie	53	12147	8	girl
Drea	22	4265	34	girl
Dream	61	2144	88	girl
Drew	110	322	1053	boy
Drew	22	1169	208	girl
Dulce	61	655	431	girl
Dulcemaria	35	5805	22	girl

E

Name	Page	Rank	Births	Gender
Eddie	146	590	463	boy
Eden	95	601	447	boy
Eden	8	151	2117	girl
Edgar	145	300	1175	boy

Name	Page	Rank	Births	Gender
Ellakate	56	7724	15	girl
Ellamae	56	3066	54	girl
Ellamarie	35, 56	4788	29	girl
Ellarae	56	7035	17	girl
Ellarose	56	5167	26	girl
Elle	56	395	818	girl
Ellen	69	656	431	girl
Ellery	79	1020	254	girl
Ellie	56	55	4442	girl
Elliemae	56	4008	37	girl
Elliot	102	217	1750	boy
Elliot	15	756	367	girl
Ellis	15	1082	234	girl
Ellison	15	897	300	girl
Elodie	85	1175	207	girl
Elsa	43	286	1131	girl
Elsie	42	336	998	girl
Elspeth	42	5632	23	girl
Elvis	139	1056	186	boy
Ember	50	435	729	girl
Emilia	79	164	1989	girl
Emiliana	47, 79	1506	145	girl
Emily	79	7	12562	girl
Emilyn	79	2434	74	girl
Emma	85	1	20799	girl
Emmagrace	51, 85	3035	55	girl
Emmajean	40, 85	5035	27	girl
Emmakate	85	9667	11	girl
Emmalene	85	6015	21	girl
Emmalia	85	7349	16	girl
Emmalina	85	4094	36	girl
Emmaline	85	880	308	girl
Emmalise	85	7733	15	girl
Emmalyn	85	465	681	girl

Name	Page	Rank	Births	Gender
George	131	134	2988	boy
Georgette	70, 86	4795	29	girl
Georgia	70, 86	243	1319	girl
Georgiana	47, 70, 86	2339	78	girl
Georgie	70, 86	4183	35	girl
Georgina	70, 86	1586	135	girl
Gerald	147	816	275	boy
Gerardo	147	402	770	boy
German	142	1156	161	boy
Gertrude	87	6483	19	girl
Gia	39	366	881	girl
Giabella	39	5639	23	girl
Giacomo	96	3460	31	boy
Gian	117	1383	122	boy
Giancarlo	119	823	272	boy
Giancarlos	119	3224	34	boy
Gianella	39	3918	38	girl
Gianfranco	119	4565	21	boy
Gianluca	119	1166	158	boy
Gianmarco	119	3919	26	boy
Gianna	39	95	3061	girl
Gianni	117	515	535	boy
Gianni	39	2435	74	girl
Gideon	98	349	928	boy
Gigi	70, 86, 92	5041	27	girl
Gil	147	3370	32	boy
Gilbert	147	894	239	boy
Gilberto	147	1019	198	boy
Gina	56, 70, 74, 86	1462	153	girl
Ginny	92	4667	30	girl
Gino	131, 152	942	223	boy
Gio	131	2574	47	boy
Gionna	39	5315	25	girl
Giorgio	131	2113	65	boy

Name	Page	Rank	Births	Gender
Harold	148	828	270	boy
Harris	148	1084	176	boy
Harrison	148	127	3184	boy
Harry	148	714	335	boy
Haven	124	1189	154	boy
Haven	51	333	1002	girl
Heaven	52	338	984	girl
Heavenly	52	1292	183	girl
Heidi	87	347	944	girl
Helen	70	404	791	girl
Helena	70, 79	502	614	girl
Hendrick	148	2365	54	boy
Hendrix	148	546	498	boy
Henrietta	87	2461	73	girl
Henrik	148	863	253	boy
Henry	148	33	9350	boy
Herbert	148	1936	74	boy
Heriberto	148	1657	92	boy
Herman	142	1954	73	boy
Hermione	70	2962	57	girl
Hernan	148	1855	79	boy
Hernando	148	12677	5	boy
Hezekiah	102	774	297	boy
Hila	51	11228	9	girl
Hilario	139, 149	3041	37	boy
Hillary	79	1324	176	girl
Hollis	38	1804	112	girl
Holly	38	449	708	girl
Honesty	57	1024	253	girl
Honey	61	3318	48	girl
Honor	127	2506	49	boy
Honor	58	1874	107	girl
Honora	59	7054	17	girl
Hope	58, 71	231	1412	girl

Name	Page	Rank	Births	Gender
Hosanna	52	2526	70	girl
Hosea	102	2147	63	boy
Houston	149	931	226	boy
Huey	149	6391	13	boy
Hugh	149	869	251	boy
Hughes	149	8322	9	boy
Hugo	149	438	689	boy

I

Name	Page	Rank	Births	Gender
Ian	117	77	5422	boy
Ignacio	131, 149	1091	174	boy
Ignatius	131	2896	40	boy
Ike	95	1738	86	boy
Iker	124	215	1787	boy
Ila	69	1202	201	girl
Ines	66	2258	82	girl
Inez	66	2838	60	girl
Ira	109	1159	160	boy
Irene	71	668	424	girl
Irina	71	2878	59	girl
Isa	43	2060	94	girl
Isaac	95	31	9868	boy
Isabeau	43	6040	21	girl
Isabella	43	4	16950	girl
Isabellamarie	35, 44	12270	8	girl
Isabelle	43	96	3044	girl
Isai	103	1130	167	boy
Isaiah	102	48	7530	boy
Isais	102	11161	6	boy
Isela	43	2769	62	girl
Ishmael	96	1283	137	boy
Isidro	149	1955	73	boy
Israel	96	240	1523	boy
Israel	9	3003	56	girl
Iva	39, 90	2061	94	girl

Name	Page	Rank	Births	Gender
Janae	40	932	286	girl
Jane	40	322	1018	girl
Janella	40	5496	24	girl
Janelle	40	450	707	girl
Janelly	40	2463	73	girl
Janet	40	1375	167	girl
Janice	40	1325	176	girl
Janie	40	1393	164	girl
Janina	40	5656	23	girl
Janine	40	4803	29	girl
Jared	96	296	1180	boy
Jaron	109	1305	134	boy
Jarrett	147, 150	1042	191	boy
Jarvis	132	1192	153	boy
Jasiah	103	630	414	boy
Jasmarie	35	9733	11	girl
Jason	112	75	5510	boy
Jasper	120	218	1731	boy
Javier	149	216	1761	boy
Javion	149	810	279	boy
Jax	117	209	1836	boy
Jaxton	118	457	640	boy
Jaycee	52	618	461	girl
Jayden	107	15	12878	boy
Jayden	18	539	569	girl
Jayna	40	1806	112	girl
JC	124	3383	32	boy
Jean	118	1063	183	boy
Jeanette	40	1947	102	girl
Jeanne	40	4281	34	girl
Jeb	108	3815	27	boy
Jebediah	108	3931	26	boy
Jedidiah	103	782	294	boy
Jemima	9	3071	54	girl

Name	Page	Rank	Births	Gender
Joel	107	154	2641	boy
Joella	18	2643	66	girl
Joelle	18	1050	245	girl
Joey	96, 112	686	364	boy
Joey	9, 24	1784	114	girl
Johan	118	579	477	boy
Johannes	118	2710	44	boy
John	118	26	10600	boy
Johncarlos	119	6788	12	boy
Johndavid	119	3816	27	boy
Johnhenry	119	6420	13	boy
Johnluke	119	2617	46	boy
Johnmichael	119	3165	35	boy
Johnny	118	299	1176	boy
Johnpaul	119	1142	164	boy
Jolie	61	790	353	girl
Jon	103	675	374	boy
Jonah	103	138	2878	boy
Jonas	103	500	558	boy
Jonathan	103	44	8035	boy
Joni	40, 87	3274	49	girl
Jordan	112	55	6810	boy
Jordana	24	2573	68	girl
Jordany	112	4938	19	boy
Jordy	131	927	228	boy
Jordyn	24	127	2533	girl
Jorge	132	207	1841	boy
José	96, 112	76	5442	boy
Joseangel	112, 121	3310	33	boy
Joseantonio	112	4582	21	boy
Josecarlos	112	7761	10	boy
Josefina	9, 24	2438	74	girl
Joseluis	112	1740	86	boy
Josemanuel	112	3166	35	boy

Name	Page	Rank	Births	Gender
Josemaria	112	4286	23	boy
Josemiguel	112	4423	22	boy
Joseph	96, 112	20	11995	boy
Josephine	9, 24	147	2255	girl
Josette	9, 24	3139	52	girl
Josh	99	1148	163	boy
Joshua	99	25	10764	boy
Josiah	103	64	6376	boy
Josiah	16	10427	10	girl
Josie	9, 24	254	1269	girl
Josue	99	269	1359	boy
Journey	52	291	1110	girl
Jovan	118	1122	168	boy
Jovanna	41	4284	34	girl
Jovanni	117	943	223	boy
Jovie	71	1365	169	girl
Jovita	71	12363	8	girl
Joy	61	462	687	girl
Joyce	87	797	349	girl
Juan	118	98	3887	boy
Juana	41	1915	104	girl
Juancarlos	119	1696	89	boy
Juandiego	119	3714	28	boy
Juanita	41	2299	80	girl
Juanito	118	6427	13	boy
Juanjose	119	3715	28	boy
Juanpablo	119	1721	87	boy
Jubilee	61	1394	164	girl
Judah	97, 104	243	1514	boy
Judah	9, 16	4285	34	girl
Jude	112	162	2564	boy
Jude	25	1795	113	girl
Judith	9, 20	952	279	girl

Name	Page	Rank	Births	Gender
Judson	112	960	218	boy
Judy	9, 20	1505	146	girl
Jules	71	2226	84	girl
Julia	71	86	3578	girl
Julian	132, 139	47	7611	boy
Julian	71	4810	29	girl
Juliana	71	157	2045	girl
Julianne	71	901	299	girl
Julianny	71	12371	8	girl
Juliano	132	3472	31	boy
Julie	71	409	776	girl
Juliet	72	258	1263	girl
Julieta	72	961	276	girl
Julieth	72	3275	49	girl
Julio	132, 139	452	650	boy
Julionna	71	9170	12	girl
Julissa	71	499	617	girl
Julius	132, 139	309	1119	boy
Junia	25	4380	33	girl
Justice	127	531	518	boy
Justice	58	421	756	girl
Justin	127	96	3991	boy
Justina	58, 72	2923	58	girl
Justine	58, 72	1964	101	girl
Justino	127	7769	10	boy
Justo	112, 127	6793	12	boy
Justus	112	819	274	boy

K

Name	Page	Rank	Births	Gender
Kai	132	177	2387	boy
Kaitlyn	72	158	2044	girl
Kalena	72	2704	64	girl
Karen	72	492	630	girl
Karla	87	504	614	girl
Katalina	67	823	334	girl

Name	Page	Rank	Births	Gender
Kate	72	207	1611	girl
Kateri	91	2845	60	girl
Katerina	73	1180	206	girl
Katherine	72	83	3651	girl
Kathleen	72	674	418	girl
Kathy	72	1547	140	girl
Katia	73	1627	131	girl
Katie	72	280	1149	girl
Katrina	73	1101	230	girl
Kay	72	2847	60	girl
Kayla	18, 21, 52	102	2982	girl
Keira	88	228	1459	girl
Kelis	10, 88	1916	104	girl
Ken	150	1771	84	boy
Kenan	97	1478	109	boy
Kenneth	150	191	2128	boy
Kenny	150	839	264	boy
Keren	10	1797	113	girl
Kesha	52	15514	6	girl
Kevin	150	70	5859	boy
Keziah	10	1452	155	girl
Khloe	23	88	3518	girl
Kian	150	494	565	boy
Kieran	150	576	480	boy
Killian	150	516	535	boy
Kingdavid	101	6449	13	boy
Kirk	124	1542	103	boy
Kirsten	52	1295	183	girl
Kit	72	7430	16	girl
Klaus	139	3943	26	boy
Knight	127	2760	43	boy
Knowledge	127	1993	71	boy
Konstantinos	138	2512	49	boy
Krista	52	1761	117	girl

Name	Page	Rank	Births	Gender
Kristen	52	814	338	girl
Kyrie	124	505	554	boy
Kyrie	52	1376	167	girl

L

Name	Page	Rank	Births	Gender
Labella	60	6083	21	girl
Lael	10	2882	59	girl
Laina	69	1764	116	girl
Lainey	69	585	511	girl
Lana	61	351	934	girl
Landry	150	829	270	boy
Landry	88	981	269	girl
Larissa	73	1094	232	girl
Larry	132	510	541	boy
Lars	132	1822	81	boy
Laura	88	318	1038	girl
Laurent	132	6844	12	boy
Laurie	88	3010	56	girl
Law	132	11477	6	boy
Lawrence	132	462	628	boy
Lawson	132	485	574	boy
Lawton	132	3112	36	boy
Lazaro	113	1857	79	boy
Lazarus	113	1371	124	boy
Leah	10	35	5563	girl
Leander	151	2075	67	boy
Ledger	151	1083	177	boy
Legacy	128	3241	34	boy
Legacy	52	1918	104	girl
Lemuel	104	2017	70	boy
Len	151	5851	15	boy
Lena	56	279	1156	girl
Lenny	151	1610	96	boy
Lenora	69	1594	134	girl
Leo	133, 139	97	3936	boy

Name	Page	Rank	Births	Gender
Lisa	43	750	371	girl
Lisamarie	35, 44	9831	11	girl
Liz	44	2709	64	girl
Liza	43	1709	122	girl
Lizbeth	44	751	370	girl
Lizeth	44	1348	173	girl
Lizette	44	2468	73	girl
Lizzie	44	2852	60	girl
Lois	25	1988	99	girl
Lola	33	236	1370	girl
Loren	132	1921	75	boy
Lorenzo	133	227	1628	boy
Loretta	88	1322	177	girl
Lottie	84	2611	67	girl
Lou	151	3830	27	boy
Louie	151	1107	171	boy
Louis	151	289	1212	boy
Louisa	91	973	271	girl
Louise	91	1219	199	girl
Lourdes	33	2028	96	girl
Love	58, 64, 73	1661	127	girl
Lovella	58	7861	15	girl
Lovely	62	2262	82	girl
Lovie	58	10522	10	girl
Loyal	128	2180	62	boy
Loyal	58	4935	28	girl
Loyalty	128	5343	17	boy
Loyalty	58	2486	72	girl
Luca	113	185	2291	boy
Luca	25	2612	67	girl
Lucas	113	19	12078	boy
Lucero	53	1679	125	girl
Lucia	73	230	1421	girl
Lucian	133	608	437	boy

Name	Page	Rank	Births	Gender
Luciana	73	469	670	girl
Lucienne	73	4491	32	girl
Lucila	73	7126	17	girl
Lucille	73	343	966	girl
Lucina	73	6291	20	girl
Lucinda	73	1522	143	girl
Lucius	113	1385	122	boy
Lucky	62	9835	11	girl
Lucy	73	62	4257	girl
Luella	91	1509	145	girl
Luigi	152	2464	51	boy
Luis	152	99	3879	boy
Luisangel	121, 152	3171	35	boy
Luke	113	28	10431	boy
Lula	91	2166	87	girl
Lulu	62	3191	51	girl
Lupita	33	1862	108	girl
Luther	157	1611	96	boy
Luz	33	1076	236	girl
Lydia	25	84	3609	girl
Lyra	88	1042	247	girl

M

Name	Page	Rank	Births	Gender
Mabel	64, 89	669	424	girl
Maci	25	263	1235	girl
Mack	133	803	283	boy
Maddie	25, 26	1151	215	girl
Madeline	25	89	3409	girl
Madelyn	25	59	4289	girl
Madison	26	9	10247	girl
Madonna	33	15679	6	girl
Magali	26	2650	66	girl
Magaly	74	2101	91	girl
Magda	26	9848	11	girl
Magdalena	26	976	270	girl

Name	Page	Rank	Births	Gender
Magdalene	26	1636	130	girl
Maggie	73	239	1344	girl
Magnus	133	977	213	boy
Maia	29	626	454	girl
Maire	29	11471	9	girl
Maisie	74	658	431	girl
Maite	18, 35, 92	1307	180	girl
Makayla	19, 53	123	2559	girl
Malachi	107	179	2352	boy
Malie	62	8718	13	girl
Malin	26	3799	40	girl
Malina	62	1595	134	girl
Mamie	29	5359	25	girl
Manasseh	97	3947	26	boy
Mandy	64, 89	1931	103	girl
Manny	124	2135	64	boy
Manuel	124	265	1370	boy
Manuela	23, 37	2288	81	girl
Maple	62	3145	52	girl
Mara	12	695	404	girl
Marcanthony	113, 142	6867	12	boy
Marcel	113	853	259	boy
Marcella	80	1434	157	girl
Marcellus	113	1359	125	boy
Marcelo	113	741	319	boy
Marco	113	308	1121	boy
Marcoantonio	113, 142	5575	16	boy
Marcos	113	404	763	boy
Marcus	113	158	2592	boy
Margaret	74	169	1933	girl
Margarita	74	1628	131	girl
Margot	74	749	372	girl
Marguerite	74	2469	73	girl
Mari	30	2047	95	girl

Name	Page	Rank	Births	Gender
Maria	30	115	2740	girl
Mariaelena	36	6564	19	girl
Mariafernanda	35	4127	36	girl
Mariah	30	136	2383	girl
Mariaisabel	35	10560	10	girl
Marian	30	1264	189	girl
Mariana	36, 48	331	1004	girl
Mariangel	36	6844	18	girl
Maribel	35	1463	153	girl
Maribella	35	3732	41	girl
Maricruz	36	4399	33	girl
Marie	30	579	523	girl
Mariel	30	2168	87	girl
Mariela	30	1358	171	girl
Marielena	36	6304	20	girl
Marielle	30	1989	99	girl
Marietta	29	2516	26	girl
Marifer	35	10562	10	girl
Mariluz	33	18094	5	girl
Marilyn	30, 36	405	791	girl
Marin	74	1402	162	girl
Marina	74	661	430	girl
Marion	30	1539	141	girl
Mariona	30	15743	6	girl
Maris	33	3374	47	girl
Marisabel	35, 44	15744	6	girl
Marisol	33	810	341	girl
Marissa	33	473	667	girl
Marita	30	7468	16	girl
Maritza	33	1203	201	girl
Marjorie	74	721	385	girl
Mark	113	189	2161	boy
Marla	26	2232	84	girl
Marlen	26	2937	58	girl

Name	Page	Rank	Births	Gender
Marlena	26	2134	89	girl
Marlene	26	1172	208	girl
Marlon	113	747	314	boy
Marnie	74	4496	32	girl
Martha	26	735	377	girl
Martin	139, 157	262	1421	boy
Martina	74	1662	127	girl
Martino	139, 157	7861	10	boy
Marty	139, 157	2624	46	boy
Mary	30	120	2611	girl
Maryalice	36	6567	19	girl
Maryann	36, 48	1574	137	girl
Marybelle	35	9284	12	girl
Marybeth	35, 44	5364	25	girl
Maryclaire	36	10570	10	girl
Maryelizabeth	35, 44	4942	28	girl
Maryella	35	5696	23	girl
Maryellen	36	5697	23	girl
Marygrace	36, 51	5219	26	girl
Maryjane	36	1242	194	girl
Marykate	37	4400	33	girl
Marykatherine	37	8725	13	girl
Marymargaret	37	379285	12	girl
Maryrose	37	8285	14	girl
Maša	30	9868	11	girl
Massimiliano	134	6871	12	boy
Massimo	152	1447	113	boy
Mateo	114	106	3704	boy
Mathias	114	582	472	boy
Matias	114	503	556	boy
Matt	114	2206	61	boy
Mattea	26	5874	22	girl
Matthew	114	16	12809	boy
Mattie	26	958	277	girl

Name	Page	Rank	Births	Gender
Mickey	107, 124	1575	99	boy
Miguel	107, 124	146	2737	boy
Miguelangel	107, 121, 124	1470	110	boy
Mike	107, 124	970	215	boy
Mikhail	107, 124	1284	137	boy
Milagro	34	4049	37	girl
Milagros	34	1367	168	girl
Milcah	12	13993	7	girl
Millie	57	505	612	girl
Mimi	31	5373	25	girl
Mirabella	62	2712	64	girl
Mirabelle	62	2233	84	girl
Miracle	65	414	768	girl
Miriam	12, 31	305	1057	girl
Misael	108	777	296	boy
Misha	19, 53	2509	71	girl
Mishael	108	6887	12	boy
Mitchell	107, 124	504	555	boy
Mitzi	30	6854	18	girl
Miya	62	903	299	girl
Modesty	58	7893	15	girl
Moira	31	1672	126	girl
Moises	99	460	632	boy
Molly	31	122	2578	girl
Mollyann	48	18239	5	girl
Monalisa	44	12641	8	girl
Monica	80	538	572	girl
Monique	80	1977	100	girl
Morris	133	1471	110	boy
Morrison	133	2100	66	boy
Moses	99	487	573	boy

N

Name	Page	Rank	Births	Gender
Nadia	58	288	1119	girl
Nadine	58	1428	158	girl
Nancy	46	752	369	girl
Naomi	12	80	3677	girl
Natalia	38	111	2778	girl
Natalie	38	23	7061	girl
Natasha	38	644	439	girl
Nate	104, 114	1530	104	boy
Nathan	104	38	8902	boy
Nathaniel	114	94	4257	boy
Navi	117	6893	12	boy
Navi	41	3869	39	girl
Nazareth	114	3248	34	boy
Nella	82	2780	62	girl
Nelly	69	1565	138	girl
Neriah	16	929	287	girl
Nestor	134	1495	108	boy
Nettie	40, 45	8313	14	girl
Neveah	53	1001	261	girl
Nicholas	139	57	6713	boy
Nick	139	1182	156	boy
Nico	140	456	644	boy
Nicola	80	4405	33	girl
Nicole	80	129	2511	girl
Nicolette	79	1530	142	girl
Nikki	80	1566	138	girl
Nikola	139	1416	118	boy
Nikolai	139	536	513	boy
Nixon	139	587	469	boy
Noa	13	941	284	girl
Noah	97	1	19144	boy
Noam	12	11590	9	girl
Noble	128	1336	129	boy

Name	Page	Rank	Births	Gender
Noble	58	9918	11	girl
Noe	96	575	481	boy
Noel	125	356	892	boy
Noelia	38	1695	124	girl
Noella	38	2304	80	girl
Noelle	38	251	1280	girl
Nohemi	12	4215	35	girl
Nora	59	49	4708	girl

O

Name	Page	Rank	Births	Gender
Obadiah	108	2019	70	boy
Obed	104	1648	93	boy
Oksana	77	6589	19	girl
Olga	89	2351	78	girl
Oliver	156	32	9365	boy
Ollie	156	1960	73	boy
Olympia	89	4597	31	girl
Ona	30	4408	33	girl
Oren	104	1616	96	boy

P

Name	Page	Rank	Births	Gender
Pablo	114	396	780	boy
Pace	128	2860	41	boy
Padraig	140	4323	23	boy
Palmer	125	1472	110	boy
Palmer	53	1349	173	girl
Paloma	53	869	312	girl
Paola	26	679	413	girl
Paolo	114	2078	67	boy
Paradise	53	4599	31	girl
Pascal	125	4620	21	boy
Pascale	53	12708	8	girl
Passion	54	4310	34	girl
Patience	59	988	267	girl

Name	Page	Rank	Births	Gender
Patrice	80	6875	18	girl
Patricia	80	739	376	girl
Patricio	140	1923	75	boy
Patrick	140	153	2658	boy
Patsy	80	7159	17	girl
Patterson	140	7366	11	boy
Patty	80	14104	7	girl
Paul	114	201	1987	boy
Paula	26	990	266	girl
Paulette	26	2267	82	girl
Paulina	26	953	279	girl
Pauline	26	2653	66	girl
Paulo	114	1942	74	boy
Pavel	114	2550	48	boy
Pax	128	2493	50	boy
Payson	27	2488	72	girl
Paz	34	7909	15	girl
Pedro	114	354	902	boy
Peggy	73	5900	22	girl
Pete	114	2079	67	boy
Peter	114	204	1899	boy
Petra	27	1524	143	girl
Philippa	27	2714	64	girl
Phillip	115	391	790	boy
Philomena	74	2715	64	girl
Phineas	99	1531	104	boy
Phoebe	27	298	1086	girl
Pia	59	2511	71	girl
Pierce	115	470	616	boy
Pierce	27	9931	11	girl
Pierre	115	1005	203	boy
Pierson	115	1301	135	boy
Pietro	114	4068	25	boy
Pilar	34	2810	61	girl

Name	Page	Rank	Births	Gender
Remi	89	662	429	girl
Remy	152	621	424	boy
Rena	54	2268	82	girl
Renata	54	659	431	girl
Renato	125	2441	52	boy
René	125	796	286	boy
Renée	54	962	276	girl
Renzo	133	2118	65	boy
Rhoda	27	3808	40	girl
Ria	30	1978	100	girl
Ricardo	153	256	1457	boy
Rich	153	5390	17	boy
Richard	153	141	2857	boy
Richie	153	1924	75	boy
Rick	153	1711	88	boy
Ricky	153	519	534	boy
Rico	153	1216	150	boy
Rita	74, 89	1382	166	girl
Rob	153	6195	14	boy
Robbie	153	2208	61	boy
Robert	153	61	6572	boy
Roberto	153	343	959	boy
Robertson	153	10407	7	boy
Robin	153	1050	188	boy
Robinson	153	2185	62	boy
Robson	153	13557	5	boy
Rocco	153	449	652	boy
Rocio	34	2022	97	girl
Rock	153	4795	20	boy
Rocky	153	990	208	boy
Roderick	154	1080	178	boy
Rodolfo	154	945	222	boy
Rodrigo	154	488	571	boy
Roger	154	584	472	boy

Name	Page	Rank	Births	Gender
Rogers	154	10409	7	boy
Roland	154	612	433	boy
Romeo	125	341	962	boy
Romy	37	2782	62	girl
Ron	154	2209	61	boy
Ronald	154	397	780	boy
Ronaldo	154	1162	160	boy
Ronan	154	366	858	boy
Ronnie	55, 90	3382	47	girl
Ronny	154	1891	77	boy
Roque	153	4201	24	boy
Rosalia	90	1742	119	girl
Rosalie	90	310	1047	girl
Rosamaria	37	9953	11	girl
Rosanna	48	2368	77	girl
Rosario	34	2290	81	girl
Rose	92	194	1678	girl
Roseann	48	9955	11	girl
Rosemary	37	575	529	girl
Rosie	92	844	324	girl
Rowan	154	239	1531	boy
Rowan	90	412	770	girl
Ruben	97	357	889	boy
Rudolph	154	2593	47	boy
Rudy	154	866	253	boy
Rue	13	4607	31	girl
Rufus	134	4798	20	boy
Rupert	155	5616	16	boy
Ruth	13	315	1042	girl
Ruthanne	48	8806	13	girl
Ruthie	13	1875	107	girl
Ryker	153	151	2666	boy

S

Name	Page	Rank	Births	Gender
Sabella	43	2752	63	girl
Sabina	75	1969	101	girl
Sabine	75	2032	96	girl
Sadie	11	46	4823	girl
Sage	128	654	399	boy
Sage	59	388	834	girl
Saint	136	3413	32	boy
Salem	105	1503	107	boy
Salem	16	1541	141	girl
Sally	11	1167	209	girl
Salome	27	1970	101	girl
Salvador	125	600	448	boy
Salvatore	125	899	237	boy
Sam	105	533	516	boy
Samantha	13	33	5680	girl
Samara	21	631	450	girl
Samaria	16	2049	95	girl
Sammy	105	1248	143	boy
Samson	99	628	416	boy
Samuel	105	23	10859	boy
Sandra	75	800	348	girl
Sandy	75	1638	130	girl
Santa	78	16051	6	girl
Santana	120	887	242	boy
Santana	45	1937	103	girl
Santi	136	7412	11	boy
Santiago	120	115	3417	boy
Santina	78	5724	23	girl
Santino	136	632	414	boy
Santos	136	909	235	boy
Sarabeth	44	6889	18	girl
Sarah	11, 20	50	4647	girl
Sarahi	11	1046	246	girl

Name	Page	Rank	Births	Gender
Sarai	11	447	710	girl
Sasha	129	4803	20	boy
Sasha	75	569	535	girl
Saul	105	447	659	boy
Savion	156	1426	117	boy
Savior	125	5621	16	boy
Seamus	115	900	237	boy
Sean	118	193	2107	boy
Sebastian	134	34	9237	boy
Sebastiano	134	5175	18	boy
Sela	13	4318	34	girl
Selah	21	545	563	girl
Semaj	115	964	217	boy
Semaj	27	3021	56	girl
Sephora	14	2892	59	girl
Seraphina	54	1335	175	girl
Serena	63	455	696	girl
Serene	63	2370	77	girl
Serenity	63	60	4284	girl
Serge	155	5907	15	boy
Sergey	155	6208	14	boy
Sergio	155	307	1138	boy
Seth	97	250	1490	boy
Shane	118	277	1282	boy
Sharon	21	879	309	girl
Shawna	41	3740	41	girl
Shayla	75	746	373	girl
Shayna	21	1731	120	girl
Shayne	41	3344	48	girl
Sheila	68, 75	1416	160	girl
Shepherd	125	1176	157	boy
Sherry	65	2784	62	girl
Shiloh	99	1051	188	boy
Shiloh	13	609	472	girl

Name	Page	Rank	Births	Gender
Shoshana	20, 28	1800	113	girl
Shyla	75	1423	159	girl
Siani	41	7190	17	girl
Sid	134	4079	25	boy
Sidney	134	1145	164	boy
Silas	115	137	2900	boy
Simeon	97	1101	172	boy
Simon	97, 115	231	1602	boy
Simona	28	2659	66	girl
Simone	28	728	381	girl
Sincere	128	624	420	boy
Sincere	59	2536	70	girl
Siobhan	41	3087	54	girl
Sol	63	2105	91	girl
Solange	90	3742	41	girl
Soledad	33	4320	34	girl
Soleil	63	1470	152	girl
Solomon	105	380	813	boy
Sonia	75	946	282	girl
Sonny	136	891	241	boy
Sophia	75	3	18490	girl
Sophiagrace	51, 75	8375	14	girl
Sophiamarie	37, 75	8376	14	girl
Sophiarose	75	10752	10	girl
Sophie	75	91	3364	girl
Sophina	75	8840	13	girl
Sparkle	63	6614	19	girl
Stacy	49, 66	1205	201	girl
Steele	128	1651	93	boy
Stefan	135	851	260	boy
Stefano	135	2387	54	boy
Stella	34	66	4165	girl
Stellarose	34	8844	13	girl
Stephania	76	5119	27	girl

Name	Page	Rank	Births	Gender
Torianna	48	16242	6	girl
Treasure	65	1051	245	girl
Trina	73	5123	27	girl
Trinity	55	110	2781	girl
Trisha	80	1657	128	girl
Trixie	67	11770	9	girl
Tru	128	2022	70	boy
Tru	59	3975	38	girl
Trudy	87	6917	18	girl
Truett	128	1664	92	boy
Truly	59	3387	47	girl
Truman	128	961	218	boy
Truth	128	3199	35	boy
Truth	59	5570	24	girl

U

Name	Page	Rank	Births	Gender
Unique	63	1504	147	girl
Unity	55	6629	19	girl
Urban	140	4216	24	boy
Uriah	105	506	554	boy
Uriel	109, 120	490	570	boy
Urijah	105	788	292	boy
Uziel	99	2080	67	boy

V

Name	Page	Rank	Births	Gender
Valentin	135	980	212	boy
Valentina	76	112	2769	girl
Valentine	135	2960	39	boy
Valentine	76	3453	46	girl
Valentino	135	765	305	boy
Valor	128	2412	53	boy
Van	117	773	300	boy
Vanessa	19	171	1913	girl
Vania	39	2896	59	girl
Vanna	39	4324	34	girl

Name	Page	Rank	Births	Gender
William	156	5	16687	boy
Willie	156	722	331	boy
Wilson	156	594	459	boy
Winifred	90	1995	99	girl
Winnie	90	1417	160	girl
Wisdom	59	3750	41	girl
Wolf	156	2601	47	boy
Wolfgang	156	1653	93	boy

X

Name	Page	Rank	Births	Gender
Xander	135	211	1824	boy
Xavi	156	1128	168	boy
Xavier	156	88	4726	boy
Xenia	77	4326	34	girl
Ximena	28	142	2323	girl

Y

Name	Page	Rank	Births	Gender
Yadiel	109	1075	179	boy
Yael	100	910	235	boy
Yael	13	1853	109	girl
Yahaira	14	2720	64	girl
Yahir	100	564	489	boy
Yana	39	2122	90	girl
Yanet	40	4424	33	girl
Yudith	9, 20	9446	12	girl
Yves	149	8706	9	boy
Yvette	90	1413	161	girl
Yvonne	90	1682	125	girl

Z

Name	Page	Rank	Births	Gender
Zachariah	108	450	652	boy
Zachary	116	82	5137	boy
Zack	108, 116	1286	137	boy
Zaneta	40	16349	6	girl
Zavion	156	1373	124	boy

Name	Page	Rank	Births	Gender
Zebulon	97	3981	26	boy
Zeke	108	736	321	boy
Zelie	82	5412	25	girl
Zenaida	77	3887	39	girl
Zephaniah	105	1380	123	boy
Zion	105	255	1471	boy
Zion	17	911	295	girl
Zipporah	14	2398	76	girl
Ziva	21	1518	144	girl
Zoey	11, 55	22	7358	girl
Zofia	75	2247	83	girl
Zuri	59	475	660	girl
Zuriel	100	1666	92	boy

Made in the USA
Middletown, DE
07 August 2022

70756189R00126